The Sociology of Marx

The
SOCIOLOGY
of
MARX

Henri Lefebvre

Translated from the French by
Norbert Guterman

COLUMBIA UNIVERSITY PRESS
New York

Library of Congress Cataloging in Publication Data

Lefebvre, Henri 1905–
The sociology of Marx.

Translation of: Sociologie de Marx.
Reprint. Originally published: New York:
Pantheon Books, 1968.
Includes bibliographical references and index.
1. Communism and society.   2. Marx, Karl, 1818–1883.
I. Title
HX542.L3813   1982   301   82-9539
ISBN 0-231-05580-3
ISBN 0-231-05581-1 (pbk.)

Library of Congress Catalog Number: 68-10253

Columbia University Press Morningside Edition 1982
Columbia University Press
New York

Clothbound editions of Columbia University Press books are Smyth-sewn and
printed on permanent and durable acid-free paper.

Contents

Preface to the Morningside Edition

This book, already several years old, concerns a body of work now more than a century old: the writings of Karl Marx. It raises the question whether today we must study Marx as we study Plato, or rather whether Marx's work retains a contemporary value and significance; in other words, whether his work contributes to an elucidation of the contemporary world. Does Marx's work continue to hold for us a historical interest and only a historical interest? Does it represent but an isolated episode in the history of thought and knowledge? Is its importance then only cultural? Or does it remain a key—perhaps even *the* key—to an understanding of modern societies and modern reality?

This book's fundamental thesis still stands. It can be stated as follows: "Marx was neither a philosopher, nor an economist, nor a historian, nor a sociologist. Yet within his work one finds responses to various problems of philosophy, as well as to those of particular specialized fields (economics, history, sociology, anthropology, etc.)." How is this so, and why? Marx's thought is global: it achieves, even constitutes, a totality. Marx was no philosopher in the classic sense of the term; in effect, he desired to go beyond the philosophical because he wanted to alter the quality of life and the social order, rather than merely being content with understanding and interpreting them. Yet Marx retains philosophy's need for a coherent whole, bringing together practical experience, acquired knowledge, and anticipations of the future, that is, of the possible. Similarly, Marx was not an economist, despite certain dogmatic and widely popular interpretations of his work; on the contrary, he produced a critique both of economy and of economics. A historian? Yes, in a sense, since his method first requires a return backward in time, followed by a reciprocal and inverse progression, a movement that reconstructs the origins of contemporary reality. This process, referred to as "historical materialism," is too often reduced to a simplified historicism. As a concept, however, it is bound up with very general ideas concerning the role of historical conflicts and contradictions, ideas incontestably philosophical in origin but which Marx judges to be confirmed by experience. A sociologist? In analyzing the society of his era, Marx studies precisely those objective and subjective realities which are incorporated into the realm of that differentiated and specialized field of knowledge known as sociology: the family, nationality and the nation, political representations and the strategies of various class struggles, etc. He does not, however, carve out of reality (as one does today) an epistemological field bearing the name "sociology." On the contrary, Marx would repudiate any such delimitation that stands in the way of global apprehension and comprehension. The same is true for anthropology. Yet one must realize that Marx's analyses in this area date from his so-called youthful work, especially the celebrated "1844 Manuscripts," somewhat disdained by Marxists of certain tendencies since these works have not always been read and studied in a larger context.

One cannot, however, avoid the fact that the notion of "totality" is difficult to define and even more difficult to employ. Many Marxist theoreticians (including Lukács and Althusser) have failed in this undertaking because of their tendency to use this idea dogmatically. One cannot deny that Marx received this idea from Hegel and, through him, from the philosophical tradition. Marx himself does little to clarify it. The efforts of numerous commentators have obscured it more than they have explained it. Moreover, the idea has drifted toward the notion of *system;* but there is no Marxist system. Marx's thought does not close itself off; it remains open simultaneously to knowledge and discoveries, to practical action and political action, to the furthering and deepening of theory. An open system? In a sense, one can say so. But this label overlooks the profound originality of Marx's work, reducing his thought to considerations and definitions in which he would not recognize himself. In fact, Marx's work engages a *multi-* or *pluri-dimensional* conception of time and space, of origins and the present moment, of the possible and of the future. An understanding of this, inherent in *The Sociology of Marx,* still does not respond, however, in a totally satisfactory way, to several questions: "Where today is Marx's totality evident? Might it be found in the mode of production, that is, capitalism, which has been developing for a century despite, or perhaps by means of, conflicts and contradictions? How, according to Marx's dialectical schema, can a totality contain—that is, at once conceal and recover active contradictions? Could not today's idea of the "total" be that of the worldwide and, foremost, the worldwide commerce for which Marx only sketched a theory? Or perhaps the "total" could be the critical state in which all contemporary societies find themselves? Does not this critical state totalize the aspects and elements of the entire planet in such a way that it may become what Marx, after Hegel, calls the labor of negativity—of *crisis*—which now permits us to conceive of totality?" This latter hypothesis today seems the most probable. In this volume this hypothesis is present only implicitly, not explicitly, since it was only formulated in recent years, those of the global crisis!

The reader will thus find here some reflective, almost unprecedented themes that do not abolish the sociological study of Marx but rather situate that study in a new light. Moreover, it is true that since Marx's time the specialized sciences have developed and even been legitimized. Within the human and social experiences, knowledge has bearing upon the genesis of the "real" and upon the *differences* which it conceals. Let us take, for example, what is called the *social*. It is not always easy to define it as the proper object of sociology or as the domain of sociological research. The social cannot be confused with the economic and the political. The frequent confusion and brutal hierarchization of these "levels" have grave consequences for both theory and practice; they lead, in effect, to the obscuring, devalorization, and even the collapse of the social as such. At least in Europe and France, these positions have led more than one sociologist to an autocritique, obliging him to state explicitly the goal and method of this discipline.

One must emphasize that the fragmentation of specialized fields cannot continue indefinitely under the pretext of rigor and precision. Today, the work of many researchers demonstrates a need for generalities, a need which epistemological reflection desires to satisfy but which it is insufficient to allay. An expectation of and need for unity, for synthesis and consequently for global comprehensiveness, is coming to light in those sciences called "human" as it is in those called "natural." What thus proposes itself to us, given these new circumstances, is Marx's thought and (to use a Hegelian term taken up and familiarized by Marxists) his sociological "moment."

Henri Lefebvre
May 1982
(translated by William Germano)

The Sociology of Marx

I

Marxian Thought and Sociology

This brief study grew out of what we have referred to elsewhere[1] as "a new reading of Marx." What we have in mind is not another "interpretation," but first and foremost an attempt to reconstruct Marx's original thought. The attempt seems worth making in view of the divergencies and contradictions that have marked the development of "Marxist" thought in our time.

To define the purpose of this book more closely, we shall begin by recalling Marx's conception of the dialectical movement of reality and truth. Our conclusions will come back to this point of departure. In between we will analyze the hypotheses involved in greater detail and develop a number of themes:

a. The "truth of religion"—what religion really is—is discovered in philosophy. This means that philosophy contributes a radical criticism of religion, that it lays bare the essence of religion, namely, the initial and fundamental alienation of the human creature, root of all alienation, and that it can demonstrate how this alienation came about. This particular truth was arrived at gradually, in the course of long and bitter struggles. Born of religion, philosophy grows up in ground religion has prepared and battles hard against it, not always victoriously.

b. The truth of philosophy—what philosophy really is—is discovered in politics. Philosophical ideas—views of the world, of society, and of man elaborated by philosophers—have always been related in some way to political issues and goals. This has been so whether the philosophers took their stand for or against the powers that be. A cultivated human reason arises in two contradictory yet closely linked ways: as *raison d'état* (law, the state's organizational capacity, its ideological power), and as philosophical reason (organized discourse, logic, systematic thought). This long philosophical and political development culminates in the perfect philosophical-political system: Hegelianism. Its very perfection brings about its disintegration. The radical critique which accomplishes this salvages still usable bits and pieces from the wreckage: specifically, the method (logic and dialectics) and certain concepts (totality, negativity, alienation).

c. Now, are politics and the state self-sufficient? Do they contain and control the truth of the reality that is history? Marx denies this Hegelian thesis. The truth of politics, and hence of the state, he maintains, is to be found in society: social relationships account for political forms. They are the living, active relationships among people (groups, classes, individuals). Contrarily to what Hegel thought, what he called "civil society" has more truth and more reality than political society. To be sure, these social relationships do not exist in some substantial, absolute fashion, they do not subsist "in the air." They have a material foundation—the productive forces, that is to say, tools and machines, also the way the work is organized. Tools and techniques, however, are used and are effective only within the framework of a social division of labor, are directly dependent on the social conditions of production and ownership, on the existing social groups and classes (and their conflicts). These active relationships taken as a whole make it possible to delimit the concept of *praxis* (social action).

This dialectical theory of truth and reality is inseparable from a given society's actual conduct of life. Both theory and practice are based upon one essential idea, that of "overcoming," of "going beyond"—it is this that unites them because this "going beyond" is at once theoretical and practical, real and ideal, is determined by both past and present activity. The Marxian "going beyond" entails a critique of the completed Hegelian synthesis: the latter in effect eliminates dialectical movement, historical time, and practical action. Religion can and must be overcome: it has been overcome in and through philosophy. The overcoming of religion means its disappearance: religious alienation, the root of all alienation, will be eradicated. The process of going beyond philosophy differs from the overcoming of religion: it is more complex. Against the traditional philosophies (including materialism with its emphasis on the abstract "thing") we must first of all rehabilitate the world of the senses, rediscover their richness and meaning. This is

what is usually called Marx's "materialism." The speculative, systematic, abstract aspects of philosophy are rejected. But philosophy does not just vanish as if it had
never been. It leaves behind it the spirit of radical criticism, dialectical thought which grasps the ephemeral
side of existence, dissolves and destroys it—the power of
the negative. Besides leaving us a certain number of
concepts, it opens up the possibility of a full flowering of
human potentialities—reconciliation of the real and the
rational, of spontaneity and thought, and the appropriation of human and extra-human nature. Man has an "essence," but this essence is not something given once and
for all, a biological and anthropological datum going
back to the earliest manifestations of humanity. It is a
developing thing; more than that, it is the essential core,
the quintessence of the actual process of historical development.

The human species has a history: like any other
reality, "generic" man comes into being gradually. Philosophers have formulated the essence of man in several
different ways; they have also played a part in developing it, in constituting it, by singling out certain crucial
features which sum up social development. Philosophers
proved incapable of realizing this philosophical project
which in any case was incompletely and abstractly formulated. Consequently, to go beyond philosophy means
to bring this project to realization, and at the same time
to put an end to philosophical alienation. In the course
of its sometimes acute conflicts with the state and political society, with all the forms of alienation (each of
these presenting itself as an immutable, eternal essence
—religion, politics, technology, art, etc.), philosophy is
brought down to earth, becomes "worldly," sheds its

philosophical form. It realizes itself in the world, it becomes the world's actual doing and making.

Going beyond politics implies the withering away of the state and the transfer of its functions, also of the rationality it monopolizes (on which it superimposes its own interests, those of the government and the bureaucracy), to organized social relationships. More precisely, democracy holds the key to what is true about all political forms: they all lead to democracy, but democracy lives only by struggling to preserve itself, and by going beyond itself toward a society freed from the state and from political alienation. The rationality that is immanent in social relationships, despite their conflicts or rather in so far as these conflicts are stimulating and creative, is thus salvaged. The management of things will replace the coercive power of the state over people.

And so we come to a fundamental idea. Social relations (including juridical relations of ownership and property) constitute the core of the social whole. They structure it, serve as intermediary (that which "mediates") between the foundation or "substructure" (the productive forces, the division of labor) and the "superstructures" (institutions, ideologies). Though they do not exist substantially in the manner of things, it is they that have proved the most enduring over the ages. They render possible a future reconstruction of the individual on new foundations, so that he will no longer be negated, reduced to an abstract fiction, or driven back upon a self cut off from other selves. The immanent rationality which has been constituted and developed in the course of historical struggles between peoples, nations, classes, and groups, will be able to grow and bloom. Praxis is not confined to this rationality. In the broadest sense, praxis also includes the action of forces alien to man, those of alienation and alienated reason, i.e., ideologies. Neither the irrational nor the creative capacities that go beyond the rationality immanent in social life dare be left out of account. Nevertheless, this rationality, with its problems, its glaring gaps, and its potentialities, lies at the core of praxis.

When we get to the very heart of Marx's thought (which he took over from Hegel, transforming it), what we find is a search for an over-all thesis concerning the relation between human activity and its accomplishments. We recognize the philosophical problem of the relation between subject and object, freed of abstract speculative trappings. To Marx, the "subject" is always social man, the individual viewed in his actual relationships with groups, classes, society as a whole. The "object" to him is the products of nature, the productions of mankind, including techniques, ideologies, institutions, artistic and cultural works. Now, man's relations with that which he produces by his unaided efforts are twofold. On the one hand he realizes himself in them. There is no activity that does not give form to some object, that does not have some issue or result which its author enjoys directly or indirectly. On the other hand—or rather, at the same time—man loses himself in his works. He loses his way among the products of his own effort, which turn against him and weight him down, become a burden. At one moment, he sets off a succession of events that carries him away: this is history. At another moment, what he has created takes on a life of its own that enslaves him: politics and the state. Now his own invention dazzles and fascinates him: this is the power of ideology. Now the thing he has produced with his own hands—more accurately, *the abstract thing*—tends to turn him into a thing himself, just another commodity, an object to be bought and sold.

In short, individual and social man's relation to objects is one of otherness and alienation, self-realization and loss of self. Hegel had grasped this twofold process, but incompletely and imperfectly, getting his terms turned around or upside down. Marxian thought rectifies the distortion, puts human thought, human history (which Hegel understood, but "upside down") "back on its feet." Hegel viewed the process whereby products, goods, works are created as a process of alienation in which man's activity is swallowed up in the object; he viewed the alienating factor, namely, the abstractness of the thing created, as a product of human consciousness, of man reduced to mere consciousness of himself.

As for the process of disalienation, Hegel conceived of it one-sidely and speculatively. According to him, disalienation is achieved by philosophical awareness. According to Marx, it is achieved in the course of actual struggles, i.e., on the practical plane, and theory is but one means (element, stage, intermediary), a necessary but insufficient one, in these multiple, multiform struggles. Thus a specific alienation can be clearly defined only with reference to a possible disalienation, i.e., by showing how it can be overcome actually, by what practical means. The worst alienation is the blocking up of development.

This dialectical movement with its three fundamental concepts of truth, going beyond, and disalienation characterizes every aspect of Marx's writings, the order in which they were written, their inner logic, the very movement of his thought.

The critical attitude, the negative "moment" or stage, is fundamental to cognition. There can be no cognition without a critique of received ideas and existing reality, particularly in the social sciences. According to Marx, the foundation of all criticism is criticism of religion. Why? Because religion sanctions the separation of man from himself, the cleavage between the sacred and the profane, between the supernatural and nature.

"The critique of religion is the prerequisite of all criticism. . . . The foundation of this critique is the following: man makes religion, religion does not make man."[2]

Alienation is defined not only as man's losing himself in the external material world or in formless subjectivity; it is also, and above all, defined as a split between the objectifying and the subjectifying processes in the individual, so that the unity between them is destroyed. What religion is, is the consciousness of the man who has not found himself or who, struggling to find his essential reality, has lost it and gone astray. Such a man, however, is not some abstract being. He is social man: "This state, this society produces religion," a mistaken, split, isolated consciousness—"an inverted world."[3]

Philosophy claims to show the true nature of this world, and in a sense the claim is justified. Philosophy unmasks religion as the general theory of this inverted world, as its encyclopaedic guide, its popular logic, its "spiritual *point d'honneur*," and its moral justification. Philosophy liberates man from nonphilosophy, i.e., from fantastic ideas uncritically accepted. Consequently philosophy is the spiritual quintessence of its epoch.

In his doctoral thesis (1839/41) Marx had said that philosophy, essentially Promethean, rejects "all heavenly and earthly gods who do not recognize that man's consciousness is the highest divinity."[4] All the same, philosophy is no more than theory. It comes into being as the truth about the nonphilosophical world—religion, mythology, and magic—and is in turn confronted with a nonphilosophical world of a different kind—a world of practical activities, ranging from the most mundane to the political. The philosopher comes into collision with these activities. He cannot affect them, he cannot organize them, he cannot transform them. He is thus led to the view that there is something intrinsically inadequate about philosophy. As he confronts the nonphilosophical world, his philosophical consciousness is split. Nor can he do anything to prevent this. He is driven on the one hand to this or that species of voluntarism, on the other hand to positivism. Thus two opposite tendencies arise. The first upholds the concept, the principle of philosophy: this is a theoretical tendency that attempts to derive practical energy from philosophy: the mind's power of becoming an active force in the world. The attempt comes down to one of *realizing* philosophy. The other tendency criticizes philosophy, stresses man's needs and aspirations, what is actually going on in history. This is an attempt to *abolish* philosophy. These two tendencies break up the historical process, split it in two, block its development. Both involve a fundamental error. That of the first is to suppose that philosophy can be realized without being abolished itself. That of the sec-

ond is to suppose that philosophy can be abolished without being realized.[5]

Philosophy, in short, like religion before it, aims at
changing the world but the philosopher can no more
realize his ambition than the religious man can realize
his. To the extent he does realize it, he destroys himself.
Philosophy defines the nonphilosophical world the philosopher is to penetrate and transform, yet cannot penetrate it, cannot change reality into truth by its own
means. The image of man it forms cannot be made
real.

Thus there is a philosophical alienation (which
seeks to invest the world, to become historical and universal). Radical criticism shows first of all that "philosophy is merely religion translated into thought," hence
equally to be rejected as another form of the alienation
of the essence of man. "The philosophical consciousness
is merely the consciousness of the alienated world." And
"the philosopher (who is himself an abstract version of
alienated man) sets himself up as the measuring rod of
the alienated world."[6]

Actually, philosophical discussions have a political
meaning in every case, i.e., they are related in some way
to given social groups or classes, and to the conflicts
among them. Philosophy differs from religion because it
criticizes religion, from the state because its problems—
and solutions—are not directly political. However, generally speaking, philosophical ideas are those of the
dominant groups and classes. The philosophical currents
that represent the interests, goals, and prospects of the
oppressed have never been very strong, and have been
readily defeated. Philosophers, advancing motives of
their own, always came to terms with religion and the

state, but despite such compromises inevitable conflicts arose within philosophy. Worse still, the most elaborate, the most systematic, the most dogmatic philosophies were all bound up with one or another bureaucracy. For every bureaucracy possesses a system of knowledge in self-justification, which sets standards for filling its ranks and promoting its members, for legitimizing the hierarchical order.

In this view,[7] philosophical materialism is especially suitable for giving expression to the corporative and professional groups at the basis of a bureaucratized society—what is called "civil society." Spiritualism, on the other hand, is better suited for the "apparatus" of a narrowly political bureaucracy. However, there are constant mutual borrowings, encroachments, and compromises between the two.

Summing up, philosophy must be superseded, i.e., its project must be realized on the one hand, and on the other hand the philosopher's alienation, philosophical abstraction, systematized dogmatism must be rejected. Where is the truth of philosophy to be found? In the history of the state which epitomizes social struggles and social needs. The truth we are looking for is the social truth.[8] Once historical and social reality has been unmasked, philosophy loses all claim to autonomous existence; it is no longer needed. Its place would be filled by, at most, a summary of the most over-all results to be extracted from the historical development. What are these results? Let us recall them: an image of human potentialities; the methods, concepts, and spirit of a radical criticism freed of all philosophical compromises. What use, then, do they serve? They are extremely important: the philosophical heritage is not to be scorned.

Thanks to it we are enabled to lay out the historical materials in a meaningful order. Philosophy bequeaths us some valuable resources, on condition we do not, like the philosophers, expect it to supply us "with a recipe or schema within which to legitimize the setting up of historical epochs."[9] Philosophy takes us only to the point where the real problems arise: exposition of the past, the present, and the possible; a correct ordering of the materials of reality; the transformation of reality according to the potentialities it actually holds. Philosophy supplies us with some means for addressing ourselves to these problems, for formulating and solving them. In short, *via* the critical study of religion and the political state, it leads us as far as the social sciences. No farther.

Marx is still in many quarters looked upon as an economist. He is believed to have championed a certain "economic determinism," according to which the level of development of the productive forces mechanically or automatically determines the other relations and forms that constitute social life, property relations, institutions, ideas. For allegedly holding such a view he is sometimes criticized, sometimes approved. But (it should hardly be necessary to point out yet another time) this interpretation overlooks the subtitle of *Capital*, which was a "*Critique* of Political Economy." After all, wasn't it capitalism that founded itself upon economic reality: commodities, money, surplus value, profit? By contrast with capitalism, in which the mediation of money changes relations between persons into the quantitative relations that obtain between abstract things, medieval society was founded on direct relations among human beings, relations between masters and serfs—no doubt

relations of bondage, but perfectly clear ones. Once society has been transformed, human relations will again
become clear and direct, only without servility.[10] As for
political economy as a science, it is the study of a certain
praxis: how goods in short supply are distributed among
groups unequal in size, influence, function, and place in
the social structure. Political economy must be superseded, is capable of surmounting itself. This should be
achieved in and by a society living in abundance,
making full use of its technological potentialities. The
process entails the overcoming of law—that aggregate of
norms and rules governing the distribution of products
and activities in a society that has not yet achieved
abundance. Consequently, political economy is merely
the science of scarcity. To be sure, every society had and
still has an economic "foundation" or "base." This base
determines social relations, however, only to the extent
that it limits the activities of groups and individuals; it
imposes shackles on them; it arrests their potentialities
by limiting them. In giving rein to their potentialities,
individuals—as representatives of groups and classes—
undertake things on their own initiative which may or
may not succeed, but which assigns economic reality a
more complex, higher, more varied place in the social
whole. For all that, the transformation of capitalist society calls for a modification of the economic base—in the
relations of production and ownership, in the organization of work, and in the social division of labor.

Capital is a study of a specific society, namely,
bourgeois or middle-class society, and a specific mode of
production, namely, capitalism. It considers these two
aspects of one and the same reality, taken as a whole.
Competitive capitalism is here grasped theoretically the

better to be described and challenged. As a description, Marx's work deals with this society's self-regulative mechanisms, the balancing mechanisms that tend to uphold its various structures: how the average rate of profit is arrived at, how reproduction on a progressively increasing scale is proportioned. Competitive capitalism constitutes a system. Within it arises a specific *form* of the product of human labor: the commodity. The specifically capitalist relations of production and ownership determine a specific *structure* of both the productive forces and the social forces. As a challenge, this work shows how the proletariat is led to become conscious of capitalism in the course of its struggles with the bourgeoisie, the dominant class. Marx goes farther than this, and demonstrates that competitive capitalism is fated to disappear. Two socio-economic forces threaten it, tend to break up its internal structures: the working class and the monopolies (the latter resulting from the inevitable concentration and centralization of capital). In short, though *Capital* contains an economic theory, it is not a treatise on political economy. It contains something else and more important: a way of superseding political economy, through radical criticism of it. The economic or, more accurately, the *economistic* interpretation distorts this work when it cuts down its real scope to a single aspect, at the same time truncating the conceptual range of the work.

"We recognize only one science, the science of history," Marx wrote in *The German Ideology* (1845). This work, composed in collaboration with Engels, expounds the principles of so-called "historical materialism." Any "historicizing" interpretation of Marxian thought must take this as its starting point. At first glimpse, the formula just quoted seems clear. It says that history is a fundamental matter for knowledge: the science of man. However, as we scrutinize it more closely, we may wonder what Marx meant. How could he grant such a privileged status to history? And what did he mean by "history"?

Indeed, if, as proclaimed, history is the only science of human reality, how could Marx have devoted himself to economic studies? Why should he have bothered? Must we conclude that his method and outlook changed, that he shifted from historicism to economism, from one specialized science (overestimated at a certain moment) to another specialized science?

These questions are answered in the preface and afterword to *Capital*, as well as in the work itself. This work expounds the development of competitive capitalism as a whole—its formation, expansion, apogee, and inevitable disintegration. It starts from this hypothesis which the work as a whole is intended to verify: capitalist society, like any other reality, comes into being, grows, declines, and dies. This is true of natural realities, social realities, individuals, ideas, institutions. The history of competitive capitalism unfolds on many planes and at different levels. The work contains some political economy (theories of the commodity, money, rate of profit, capital accumulation, etc.); some history proper (chiefly of England, the English middle classes, and English capitalism); some sociology (pre-capitalist societies are discussed, also the bourgeois family, social classes viewed from the inside, etc.). May we not say that Marx conceived and projected a *total history*, one that history in the strict sense—history as a field of knowledge, a science—cannot encompass? History as a process and history as a science do not coincide, though they converge. By historical reality, or "historicity," we denote the process by which man is formed, what he produces (in the broadest and strongest sense) by himself, through his practical activity. Man is born of nature: he comes into being, he emerges, he asserts himself. What he becomes is a result of his own efforts, his struggles against nature and against himself. In the course of this dramatic process forms and systems make their appearance. The formation of social man, like that of biological man, is marked by periods of relative stability, relatively stable structures. These, too, are eventually drawn into the process of change, are sooner or later dissolved or destroyed, yet they endured for a time, they were part of history, and deserve to be studied for their own sake.

Man, both as individual and as member of society, thus comes to look upon himself as a historical being: his "essence" is historical and unfolds within history. He constitutes, creates, produces himself in the domain of praxis. There is nothing in him that is not a product of interaction among individuals, groups, classes, societies. The historian, however, can grasp only some aspects of this total history, though he can and should try to grasp them more and more in depth. Mankind's "socio-economic formation" (as Marx calls it) simply has too many aspects, exhibits too many differences and goes on at too many levels to be treated by a single discipline. The economist, the psychologist, the demographer, the anthropologist, all have their contributions to make. And the sociologist as well.

According to the interpretation still too widely accepted in the Soviet Union, historical materialism is a kind of general sociology, corresponding to what is so termed in capitalist countries, to be sure in a broader and truer sense. According to this "establishment" Marxism, historical materialism formulates the laws that govern all societies, the universal laws of development as applied to history—dynamic contradictions, discontinuous qualitative changes, and gradual quantitative changes.

This interpretation of Marx is one of the less satisfactory ones. For how are the universal laws of dialectics that materialist sociology would apply to social development to be conceived? There are two possibilities. Either they are held to be part of philosophy, in which case historical materialism is viewed as part of dialectical materialism, and as such open to the criticism leveled against philosophical systems in general. Then the temptation is to deduce the general features from philosophy, abstractly, dogmatically. This is regression to the theoretical level of Hegelianism, or even farther back. Alternatively, the universal laws of dialectics are linked with methodology, in which case they serve as conceptual tools for analyzing actually existing societies, no matter what contents, experiences, facts they may consist of. Concrete sociology, still to be constituted on the basis of the dialectical method Hegel elaborated and Marx transformed, would deal with contents, facts, experimental data. If so, historical materialism may be viewed as an introduction to sociology, but not as sociology! Furthermore, the thesis we are rejecting here neglects the dialectical analysis of development in all its various aspects: the processes, the contents are separated from the forms they produce, the systems, the structures. We have, on the one hand, the process of growth (considered quantitatively, economically, in terms of material production), and, on the other hand, development (considered qualitatively, socially, in terms of the progressive complexity and richness of human relations). The idea of change or becoming remains pretty crude, well-nigh metaphysical, for all the pretentious talk about concrete history, materialism, dialectics, and science.

Marx did not formulate a philosophy of history: on this score, too, he broke with Hegelianism. His originality was to conceive, as a totality, the production of man by his own efforts, his own labor, starting from nature and from need in order to achieve enjoyment (the appropriation of his own nature). Thus Marx conceived of a historical science that would avoid the limitations of narrative and institutional history. Such a science, in collaboration with other sciences, was to consider the development of man in all its aspects, at every level of his practical activity. The term "historical materialism" does not designate a philosophy of history but the genesis of mankind as a totality, object of every science of human reality and goal of action. It must be emphasized that this conception of mankind's development does not come down to a history of culture, any more than to an economic history. Moreover, Marx pointedly refrains from giving a definition of the human being. He expects mankind to define itself in praxis. How can man be separated from nature with which he maintains a dialectical relationship—unity and scission, struggle and alliance? Man's destiny is to transform nature, to appropriate it as his own, both around and inside himself.

Having discarded the economist and historicist interpretations of Marxism, are we to adopt a sociological interpretation? Are we to view Marx as a sociologist? Such an interpretation would be just as inadequate as the others, though it has been fairly widespread in Germany and Austria. It began by getting rid of the philosophy attributed to Marx, without, however, analyzing the meaning of philosophy in its full implications, and without formulating any thesis of how it is to be overcome (i.e., fully translated into practice). As a result, this interpretation arbitrarily mutilated Marx's thought, giving rise to endless discussions culminating in a new Byzantinism or Scholasticism. From this point of view, Marxism falls into line with Comte's positivism. Marxist thought is dulled, loses its cutting edge. Exercise of dialectical method gives way to the worship of "facts," critical challenge is subordinated to description. In *Capital*, the use made of the key concept of totality is never allowed to overshadow the essential dialectical contradiction. On the contrary: the principle of contradiction takes on a sharpness it had lost in Hegel's systematization; Marx keeps multiplying and emphasizing the contradictions between men and works, otherness and alienation, groups and classes, substructures and superstructures. The sociologizers, on the other hand, are led by their treatment of society as a whole to play down the contradictions. Classes and class struggles are blurred. So-called "society" is readily identified with the nation and the nation-state. This allegedly Marxian sociologism fitted only too well into the ideological and political framework Marx criticized so vigorously in his comments on the Gotha program (1875). Every positivist sociology presenting itself as "Marxist" has always tended to reformism. Hence its bad reputation among some, and its attraction for others. Today this sociology is becoming overtly conservative, whereas originally—as practiced, for instance, by Saint-Simon and Fourier, who belonged to the left wing of romanticism—it did not separate knowledge from criticism.

For quite a number of reasons, then, we shall not make a sociologist out of Marx. Anyone who ascribes such a thesis to us on the basis of the title of this little book either never opened it or is acting in bad faith. We mention the possibility because far worse things than this have occurred in the context of such discussions. *Marx is not a sociologist, but there is a sociology in Marx.*

To interpret this seemingly inconsistent statement, we must keep in mind two groups of concepts and arguments:

1 Marx asserts the unity of knowledge and reality, of man and nature, and of the social sciences and the physical sciences. He explores a totality in process of becoming and in its present stage of development, a totality comprising levels and aspects which are now complementary, now distinct, now contradictory. As such, his theory therefore is not history, not sociology, not psychology, etc., but comprehends these approaches, these aspects, these various levels of the whole. Therein lies its originality, its novelty, and its lasting interest.

Since the end of the nineteenth century, there has been a tendency to view the writings of Marx, and *Capital* especially, in terms of the individual sciences; actually, it is only since his day that they have become specialized in a system of academic compartmentalization we may be sure Marx would have opposed. *Capital,* which is theoretically all of a piece, has been reduced to a treatise on history, on political economy, on sociology, even on philosophy. Marxian thought is simply too broad in scope to fit into the narrow (and ever narrower) categories of latter-day philosophy, political economy, history, and sociology. Nor is it correct to refer to it as "interdisciplinary"—a conception recently advanced (not without risk of confusion)—to remedy the disadvantages of a latter-day division of labor in the social sciences. Marxian investigation bears upon a differentiated totality and centers around a single theme—the dialectical interrelations between men active in society and their multifarious, contradictory accomplishments.

2 The specialization and compartmentalization that have gone on in the sciences of humanity since Marx's *exposure* of competitive capitalism are not devoid of meaning. The totality of human knowledge can no longer be encompassed as it could in Marx's epoch, at once from the inside and from the outside (both as a reality and as a possibility), critically and descriptively. All the same we cannot endorse this breaking up of the social sciences. It encourages us to forget the totality: society as a whole, the totality of human efforts. Of course, human reality is growing steadily more complex, and this mounting complexity is part of history in the broader sense. We are dealing with a broken-up totality, fragments of which confront one another and sometimes separate when they do not enter into conflict—the capitalist "world," the socialist "world," the undeveloped "world," the various cultures, the diverse forms of the state. It has even been suggested that the concepts "world" and "the worldwide" might replace the concept of totality to signify the extension of technology into a planetary scale. With such questions of terminology still pending, the indispensable presuppositions in the social

sciences remain the unity of knowledge and the total character of reality. Thus it is possible to recognize in Marx's works a sociology of the family, of the city and the countryside, of subgroups, classes, and whole societies, of knowledge, of the state, etc. And this can be done at such a level of analysis and exposition as not to encroach upon the rights of the other sciences—political economy, history, demography, psychology. On the other hand, it is possible to continue Marx's own effort, starting from *Capital* and embracing its method, by inquiring into the genesis of so-called "modern" society, its fragmentations and contradictions.

2

The Marxian Concept
of Praxis

Throughout his life Marx renewed assaults on the fortress (perhaps a better metaphor would be Kafka's Castle) of Hegelianism. It had something he wanted, that was his by right. Or, to put it differently, he wanted to save what was worth saving from the wreckage of the absolute system. No doubt this matter of the exact relationship between Marx's thought and Hegel's will continue to present riddles for a long time, and to inspire research. The relationship is a dialectical one: i.e., one full of conflict. Marx in one sense continues Hegel, in another sense breaks with him; now he merely "extends," now he transforms him utterly. It was quite late in life, when he was writing *Capital*, that Marx formulated a dialectical method of his own, spelling out just how it differs from the Hegelian method. At a very early date, however, he substituted the concept of "overcoming," which he took from Hegel, for that of synthesis, which, in the construction of the Hegelian system, crowns, completes, and immobilizes thesis and antithesis.

It is no part of our present endeavor to trace point by point, topic by topic, where Marxian thought takes over or extends Hegelian thought, and where it differs radically. We shall be content to indicate the major point of dissension, the matter with reference to which Marx's thought collided head on with Hegel's. It has frequently been lost sight of since, in the course of Marxism's complex history. This was the question of the state. To Hegel, at least by the time he became philosopher of the state, the state is at once what holds society together and society's crowning achievement. Without the state, the elements that compose social reality—the "estates," the crafts and corporations, subdivisions like municipalities and families—would fly apart. Without its rules and regulations there would be a breakdown of objective morality (manners and customs, morals) and of subjective morality (sense of duty, sense of obligation) alike. Human history attains its peak in the modern constitutional state. There is nothing further to look forward to in the womb of time or to expect from human endeavor.

Marx took a diametrically opposed position. The state is just another institution dependent on historical conditions. *It* does not summon *them* into being, and then, by some metaphysical process, give *them* shape and meaning. To phrase it in terms Marx had not yet selected when he embarked on his radical criticism of Hegel's philosophy of right and of the state, institutions have a base and are themselves superstructures. As for the Hegelian thesis according to which the middle class (and the state bureaucracy bound up with it) is the "universal" class, bearer of knowledge and consciousness to all mankind, Marx flays it in the strongest possible terms.

Now, the question has to be asked: is the Marxian criticism a "theoretical" one? Yes, it is. It proceeds by analysis of concepts to the very core of theory, and beyond. But it is a fundamentally practical criticism at the same time. The trouble with the Hegelian system was that it made history culminate in the present, represented a sort of "end of history," and thereby paralyzed the hope of action. From the first, Marx *thought* as a man of *action*. His whole life was one long battle for democracy, for socialism and communism, for a better society. His initial strategy calls for an alliance with the proletariat. Why? Because the working class was flatly challenging the "truth" of the current establishment, was doubting the built-in virtue of existing institutions. He was unable to accept a philosophical system which was consecrating (in the strongest sense of the term: making holy, canonizing) the existing state and "system of rights." Now, Marx himself believed the Hegelian system to be the perfect philosophical system: *the* system. Marx's criticism of the state is intrinsically interwoven with his criticism of philosophy.

But the relationship was not just one of head-on collision. As Galileo came before Descartes, so Hegel came before Marx. We might speak of a Hegelian-Marxist revolution in the knowledge of man, but it would be more accurate to give Kant and Kantianism credit for the major shift in emphasis. What does the revolution consist in? In this, that first to Hegel and then to Marx, the object of investigation and knowledge is time. In the sciences and the conceptual thought elaborated before them space played the leading part. Needless to say, time was not altogether absent from even the most "mechanistic" thought, but there it was subordinate to and determined by the dimension of space. With Hegel, extensibility in time ("becoming") comes firmly to the fore, takes on primordiality: mankind's life is now in time, is historical, its very consciousness a succession of changing stages and shifting moments. In Marx's view, Hegel betrayed his own finest insight when he gave to understand that his philosophy was the culmination of human thought and the contemporary nation-state the end of history. This is the legacy of Hegel's that Marx takes on his own shoulders and carries much farther.

With Marx change becomes truly universal, since both nature and history are now conceived historically. Man and all things human are from now on characterized in temporal terms: work hours are counted, occupations are broken down and traced back to their source, technological changes and their progressive social effects carefully noted in detail. Marx's so-called "philosophical" works consistently pursue this analysis in historical depth, until a point is reached where they burst the categories of philosophic systematization and challenge every formalization of human life in time that is advanced as definitive. Hegel was unable to formulate a system of freedom. His system of knowledge is therefore dangerous. And yet it was Hegel who laid the foundations of historical knowledge, and this has become the foundation of all knowledge of man.

In Marx, even more explicitly than in Hegel, time

has a twofold aspect: it is at once growth and development. The "beings" that are born into the changing world with a certain degree of stability grow: that is, they increase gradually in respect of certain of their characteristics. These characteristics are quantitative, and hence measurable. At the same time and out of the same process of change, new characteristics, qualitative differences, emerge. Growth and development go hand in hand. There is a connection between them, stipulated by the most general principles (laws) of dialectical thought. A "being" that only grew quantitatively would soon turn into a monster. And yet these two aspects of the process of change differ and sometimes separate and diverge from each other. Monstrous forms of life do exist, are not at all rare, and perhaps represent a form of decline and death. Growth, then, is quantitative, continuous; development is qualitative, discontinuous. It proceeds by leaps; it presupposes them. Growth is easy to predict, development less so. It may involve unforeseeable accidents, the sudden emergence of new qualities irreducible to pre-existing qualities and determinist expectations. History is rich in fresh creations, always richer in works and forms than our knowledge allows us to predict, our reflection to expect.

When one reads Hegel in the light of Marxism, particularly the *Philosophy of Right*, the concept of praxis turns up there. In his analysis of what he calls "civil society," Hegel distinguishes it from political society (the state and its personnel: the government and the bureaucracy). Civil society includes such groups as families, crafts and occupations ("estates"), towns and other territorial groupings. The needs of its members are organized into a coherent system and are satisfied by division of labor. Civil society arises from the interaction of these elements, and is consolidated and crowned by the legal system, "the system of rights," the state, the government, the bureaucratic apparatus of the state.

The concept of praxis is and is not present in Hegel. For in his philosophico-political system the divine, providential state creates its own conditions, and these only count as materials for the juridical and political structure. Because Hegel views these elements or conditions merely as "moments," stages in the development of the higher reality of the state, without any substance of their own, he treats them as secondary.

In Marx's *Manuscripts of 1844*, the *Theses on Feuerbach*, *The Holy Family* and *The German Ideology* (written in collaboration with Engels in 1845/46), the concept of praxis is clarified.

The *Manuscripts of 1844* criticize and reject the basic categories and concepts of philosophy, including the concepts of "materialism" and "idealism." What is "substance" in the philosophical sense of the term? It is nature in metaphysical disguise, arbitrarily separated from man. Similarly, consciousness is the human mind in metaphysical disguise arbitrarily separated from nature.

Both materialism and idealism are *interpretations* of the world, and both are untenable in the face of revolutionary praxis. They are no longer opposed and hence neither is valid. The specificity of Marxism, its revolutionary character, and hence its class character, do not derive from any option for materialist assumptions, but from its *practical* character, from the fact that it goes beyond speculation, and hence beyond philosophy—beyond materialism and idealism alike. There had been interpretations of the world in earlier thought, eighteenth-century bourgeois thought, most notably. Although it is true that materialism, generally speaking, has been the philosophy of oppressed and revolutionary classes, including the middle classes, the function of the working class is a radically new one. By clearly stressing praxis (society's actual doing and making, based on industry, which makes it possible to become conscious of all human practice in history), this class leaves behind and rejects once and for all earlier interpretations of life which correspond to obsolete stages in the class struggle.

Consequently, Marxism (which theoretically clarifies the situation of the working class and gives it class consciousness at the level of theory) is not a materialist philosophy because it is not a philosophy. It is neither idealist nor materialist because it is profoundly *historical*. It makes explicit the historicity of knowledge; it elaborates the socio-economic formation of mankind in all its historicity.

Philosophy explains nothing; it is itself explained by historical materialism. Philosophy, a contemplative attitude, accepts the existing. It does not transform the world, but only interpretations of the world. The contemplative attitude, one of the remoter consequences of the division of labor, is a mutilated, a fragmentary activity. Now, the true is the whole. Philosophy cannot lay claim to being the supreme, the total activity. The results achieved by this contemplative activity are inconsistent with empirically observed facts. There are no immobile absolutes, there is no such thing as a spiritual beyond. Every absolute is a mask justifying man's exploitation by man. Philosophical abstractions in themselves have no value, no precise meaning. The true is also the concrete. The propositions of *philosophia perennis* either are tautologies without content, or receive concrete meaning from some historical, empirically verifiable content. To rise above the world by pure reflection is in reality to remain imprisoned in pure reflection. This position does not imply nominalist consequences; the universals are grounded in praxis, which is itself objective.

Marx denies the existence of several qualitatively different types of knowledge, such as philosophical knowledge on the one hand, scientific knowledge on the other. Abstract philosophical thought is justified only as abstraction from particular scientific insights, more accurately, for summing up the most general results obtained from the study of historical development.

Historical materialism is justified by the aim of restoring to human thought its active strength—a strength it had "in the beginning," prior to the division of labor, when it was directly linked to practice. But it is also justified by the "philosophical" decision not to be taken in by the illusions of the epoch and to create a truly universal doctrine.

This triple requirement (that thought should be efficacious, true, and universally human) at once writes finis to philosophy and yet represents its continuation, can still be regarded as a philosophical requirement. It is not fully developed in *The German Ideology* and *The Holy Family*, but we find it at the heart of the subjects treated, the polemics, and the criticisms contained in texts written later.

The concept of praxis comes to the fore in Marx's so-called "philosophical" texts. As we have just said, praxis is defined by being opposed to philosophy and to the philosopher's speculative attitude. Feuerbach, who rejected Hegelian philosophy in the name of a materialist anthropology, did not succeed in getting beyond the philosophical attitude. Although he emphasizes the world of sense, he overlooks the subjective aspect of sensory perception: the activity that fashions the object, that recognizes it, and itself in it. Feuerbach does not see that the object of perception is the product (or the work) of a creative activity, at once sensory and social. Because he neglects the practical-sensory activity, he all the more neglects the practical-critical, i.e., revolutionary activity.[11] In opposition to a philosophical materialism which did not take praxis into account, idealism developed the subjective aspect of human thought, but only abstractly, ignoring sensuous activity (*Theses on Feuerbach*, I). Feuerbach himself saw only the grimy workaday aspect of praxis. However, philosophical materialism has even more serious consequences. It attributes changes in mankind to changed circumstances and the effects of education, forgetting that it is men alone who change their circumstances and that educators themselves have to be educated. Hence the materialist theory tends to divide society into two parts, one of which is raised above the other. Consequently, just like idealism, materialist philosophy justifies the state, not on the pretext of organization but that of education (*Theses on Feuerbach*, III).

"The question whether human thought can arrive at objective truth is not a theoretical but a practical question. It is in praxis that man must prove the truth, that is, the reality, the exactness, the power of his thinking. The dispute over the reality or non-reality of thinking isolated from praxis is a purely scholastic question" (*Theses on Feuerbach*, ii).

The various branches of knowledge find their scope and meaning in the way they are bound up with practical activity. The "problem of knowledge" as speculative philosophers treat of it, is a false problem. Abstract logical consistency, theory divorced from social activity and practical verification, have no value whatever. The essence of man is social, and the essence of society is praxis —acts, courses of action, interaction. Separated from praxis, theory vainly comes to grips with falsely formulated or insoluble problems, bogs down in mysticism and mystification (*Theses on Feuerbach*, viii).

In these early works praxis is defined chiefly in negative terms: as that which philosophy ignores or discards, as that which philosophy is not. This is a polemical determination, although the negative serves to bring out what is essential and positive for dialectical thought. Still, the new concept is not fully elaborated. Marx has not as yet clarified it well enough to forestall certain confusions. The criterion of practice, formulated in the second of the *Theses on Feuerbach*, will later be interpreted as a total rejection of theory in favor of practicality, as adherence to empiricism and the cult of efficiency, as a kind of pragmatism. In the name of the critique of philosophy, the importance of philosophy will be lost sight of, as will also the fact that for Marx praxis involves going beyond philosophy.

Some writers hold that the social sciences (the human or behavioral sciences, among which sociology stands in the forefront) are an adequate substitute for a philosophy on its last legs. According to them, the symbols, visions, and concepts of philosophy (which they treat as equivalent) will be supplanted by formulations of empirical fact in the fields of sociology, anthropology, cultural history, etc. These thinkers will find themselves at a loss, sooner or later, when confronted by findings specific enough but fragmentary, limited in their import, such as can take on depth and range only by a return to some sort of "philosophizing" (whether admitted as such or not). Or else—it comes to the same thing—the fragmentary techniques of the specialists will promptly impel philosophers to step in and give speculative unity to the formless mass of facts, techniques, results. There will be a tug of war between positivism and philosophism, the objective and the subjective, empiricism and voluntarism.

Others maintain that Marx discovered praxis all right, and his discovery makes philosophy useless while at the same time clearing the way for realization of the philosophers' dreams. Actually the concept of praxis is more complex than that. We have noted that it involves differences, levels, polarizations, contradictions. To analyze and expound its creative power, we must take our point of departure from the universal concepts that philosophy has elaborated.

If the discovery of praxis is interpreted as the rejection of philosophy purely and simply, are we not moving toward a philosophy of praxis, pragmatism or something like it, i.e., just another philosophy, derivative of or substitute for philosophy in the old sense?

All these tendencies are to be discerned in the contemporary Marxist movement higgledy-piggledy, without elucidation of the hypotheses or their implications. Actually, for all practical purposes, official Marxism takes an empiricist, positivist attitude, under cover of a philosophical phraseology. Its full confidence goes to the sciences and technologies (the natural or physical sciences rather than the historical and social sciences). In this way, under cover of an ideologized Marxism, it comes close to endorsing a technocratic praxis. As for the philosophy of praxis formulated by A. Gramsci, it turns into the justification of one particular practice—that of the Party, the modern prince. In other words, it becomes a philosophy of Machiavellianism, bestowing the cachet of philosophy on political pragmatism.

As for G. Lukács, in his *History and Class Consciousness*, the proletariat's class consciousness replaces classical philosophy. The proletariat represents "totality" —the apprehension of reality past, present, and to come —the domain of possibility—in radical negation of existing reality.

Unfortunately no such historical consciousness is to be found in the working class anywhere in the world today—in no real individual, in no real group. It is a purely speculative construction on the part of a philosopher unacquainted with the working class. Thus it is subject to the general criticism which distinguishes between *spontaneous* (uncertain, primitive) consciousness and *political* consciousness (resulting from the fusion in action between the conceptual knowledge of scientists and scholars—i.e., intellectuals—and the spontaneous consciousness). Lukács substitutes a philosophy of the proletariat for classical philosophy. His philosophy delegates philosophical authority, the power of representing and systematizing reality, to one thinker. This perpetuates the risks and dangers of classical systematization even—and more than ever—when the thinker becomes the collective thinker! Lukács' theory of class consciousness has the same defect as the philosophy of praxis elaborated by Antonio Gramsci. Both Marxist theoreticians have conceived the *end* of philosophy without its *realization*—a very widespread error.

The discovery of praxis does away with autonomous philosophy, with speculative metaphysics. But it progresses toward the realization of philosophy only to the extent that an efficacious (revolutionary) praxis relegates to the past, along with the division of labor and the state, the opposition between the world of philosophy (the world of truth) and the nonphilosophical world (the world of reality).

For a number of reasons, some of which were present in Marx's lifetime and some of which have emerged since, but all of which are connected with the contradictory development of Marxism in our time, we believe it indispensable to provide an explication of the concept of praxis. To do this it is not enough to group together excerpts or quotations from Marx and Engels; we have also to clarify the concept in the light of modern man's experience and ordeals. Only a full exposition of the concept, of what it implies as well as of what it makes explicit, will show that it contains many sociological elements—a sociology of needs, of objects, of knowledge, of everyday life, of political life, etc.

In the reading of Marx we propose, the successive steps are gradually integrated in an ever broader and closer conception of practical (political) action. Marx never went back on his criticism of philosophy or on his concept of praxis. To the very end of his life he intended to write an exposition of the dialectical method, but he died without having carried out this project. Not only is Marx's work unfinished, even its most developed portions are insufficiently elaborated. This has contributed to no small extent to later misunderstandings of it.

An exhaustive study of the concept of praxis in Marx, assuming that such a study is possible, would involve the comparative analysis of a considerable number of texts. We are leaving this task to others, as also the task of redefining the relations between Hegel and Marx, and many other unsettled questions. Our sole purpose is to make certain confusions less likely, if not to prevent them entirely, and to show how Marx's concept of praxis leaves room for sociology in the most modern sense of the term.

a. The concept of praxis presupposes the rehabilitation of the world of sense, restoration of the practical-sensuous as called attention to above. As Feuerbach had seen, the sensuous is the foundation of all knowledge because it the foundation of Being. The sensuous is not merely rich in meaning; it is a human creation. The human world has been created by men and women in the course of their history, starting from an originary nature which is given to us already transformed by our own efforts—tools, language, concepts, signs. Wealth at once graspable and inexhaustible, the practical-sensuous shows us what praxis is. It is one continuous revelation, a disclosure so unmistakable that we need only open our eyes to perceive the enormous scope of praxis in this human creation which encompasses landscapes, cities, objects of common use, and rare objects (works of art). The unity of the sensuous and the intellectual, of nature and culture, confronts us everywhere. Our senses become our theoreticians, as Marx put it, and the immediate discloses the mediations it involves. The sensuous leads us to the concept of praxis, and this concept unfolds the richness of the sensuous.

Relations between human beings are part of this world of sense now rediscovered, revealed, recognized. For before becoming another consciousness for the conscious subject, a living being is merely an object. Precisely as a sensuous object, it enters into more or less rich and complex social relations, which reveal it as "subject," and allow it to exercise its subjective powers—activity, reflection, desire.

b. Man, the human being, is first of all a creature of need. He "is" this to a greater extent than animals are, for nearly all of them from birth onward possess means of survival in their own bodies and their immediate environment. Failing this, they simply die, individuals and species alike. In all human activities, need in general (generically) asserts itself as a condition of human life. There is nothing in human life that does not correspond to some need or does not create a need, even in the most remote reaches of culture and technology, let alone in economic life. In addition to individual needs (which are satisfied only socially), there are social needs proper and political needs, immediate needs and cultivated needs, natural needs and artificial needs. Recognition of the subjectivity of other human beings does become a human—that is, a social—fact until the point is reached where the recognition of the others' needs becomes itself a conscious need. Finally, reason, rationality at the individual and social level, does not emerge until the development of needs has progressed to the point where human communities have need of reason in their activities.

Once he makes his (at once individual and historical) appearance in the world, man, a creature of need, remains for a long time weak and unable to defend himself. It is a matter for wonder how the human species has survived, in view of how poorly a cruel Mother Nature has equipped it. In viewing man as a creature of need, did Marx—and Marxian thought—consider him the object of a special science, such as might be called "anthropolgy"? No doubt. The *Manuscripts of 1844*[12] contain an outline of anthropology, but also a number of critical remarks. Anthropology (Feuerbach's is a typical example) tends either to immerse man in nature or to separate him from it. What must be grasped, however, is man's relation of conflict with nature: unity (even at the highest point of development man is not separated from nature) and struggle (human activity wrests from nature the satisfaction of human needs, and in doing so transforms and despoils it). Man's fundamental relation to nature may legitimately be called "ontological." On the other hand, everything man does is part of a process of change, i.e., of history. We have no right to "ontologize" history any more than nature, to make a philosophy of it, and thereby to introduce another separation between the human and the natural.

Needs are thus proper matters for study in so far as they form part of the over-all development of the human species, and in so far as they stimulate the activities of man in process of becoming human. This legitimizes the introduction of concepts such as the comparative richness or poverty of needs, their diversity, the transition from the need for objects to the need for other human beings, from natural utility to human use.

Study of needs discloses an interplay of dialectical processes. Man differs from animals in this, that in order to obtain satisfaction of his needs he created tools and invented work. Need is at once act or activity and a complex relationship with nature, with other human beings, and with objects. Through his own work man controls nature and appropriates it in part. Work is not a natural activity; it is even "anti-natural" in two senses: as toil it requires effort and discipline, and it modifies nature both externally and internally. Work becomes a need. The senses develop and are refined in and through work. Needs change and become more sophisticated, as work modifies them by producing new goods or possessions. Thus man emerges from nature and yet remains unable to break away from it. Enjoyment is what reconciles man to his fundamental ties with nature. It brings momentary relief to constant struggle, sense of separation, estrangement. For need as mark of helplessness, work substitutes need as capacity for enjoyment, as the power to accomplish such and such an action. In this way man as natural being replaces his immediate, barely or scarcely differentiated unity with nature by a differentiated totality. Multiple, he runs the risk of mutilation—alienation. The Hegelian theory of the system of needs controlled by the state must be rejected as too narrow: it does not take into account the sum total of needs and the need for totality (i.e., for fulfillment, plenitude in the exercise of all activities, gratification of all desires). The process of transcending limitation, of going beyond initially given bounds, tends toward this total fulfillment.

We thus discover that all praxis rests on a twofold foundation: the sensuous on the one hand, creative activity stimulated by a need it transforms on the other. This total phenomenon (need, work, sensuous enjoyment of the sensory object) is found at every level. Work is productive—of objects and of tools for more work. But it is also productive of new needs—production needs and needs for production. New needs, in both the quantitative and qualitative sense, react on the persons who produced them. And so need gradually develops until its highest and deepest forms are reached, the subtlest and the most dangerous: desire for human presence (and presence of desire), desire for power (and power of desire). In a sense all history is characterized by the growth and development of needs (not forgetting the artificialities, perversions, and alienations). Communism merely spells out human need by carrying it to its ultimate development, freeing it from its alienations.

The goal is the supplanting of work by technology, but before this terminal point of foreseeable development can be reached work must have become a primary need. The contradiction between work and nonwork (between human effort and the means for cutting down and eventually eliminating such effort, including both machines and production techniques) is especially stimulating. Nonwork is idleness but also spontaneity of genius, the inability to work and the reward for toil. It is need *qua* privation of complete enjoyment.[13] The human species progresses from the nonwork of the animal to the nonwork of the being powerful enough to have attained technical mastery over matter, having gone beyond the relentless (and oppressed) labor of the human masses and the nonwork (idleness) of their exploiters.

c. Work is part of a dialectical process "need–work–enjoyment," within which it is one practical and historical "moment" or stage. In the course of this process it acquires its own determinations, and new processes interact with the earlier ones. Work gets broken up (division of labor). Biological, technological (determined by the tools), and social divisions of labor interact. Functions get split up; the separation between city and countryside goes hand in hand with that between intellectual work and physical work. The city usurps the managing functions, and the latter become more refined within the urban framework: planning, administrative supervision, political orientation, relations with other territorial groups. For long periods (particularly within the "Asiatic mode of production") the city lives parasitically upon the countryside, only performing nonproductive—military, administrative, political—functions. Later, especially in western Europe, the city supplants the countryside in respect of productive work; this process is especially characteristic of the capitalist period which accelerates it. This represents the end of a long historical development during which inequality of functions became more and more accentuated. Productive work (mainly agricultural) is devalued in relation to other functions, those of chiefs, elders, warriors, priests, and sorcerers. The various groups which had persisted for millennia before becoming classes fight bitterly among themselves over the scanty surplus of the society's production. As yet the privileged functions are unable to free themselves from the control of the community; they must make careful use of their prestige in order to strengthen it, play imaginary roles, sacrifice themselves to the conditions of their primacy. The state in process of emergence does not yet permit them to take "the common people" for granted. More particularly, the privileged groups are for a long time obliged, in order to justify themselves, to invent works, to build monuments, to embellish the city, to organize celebrations and festivals.

At this point one of the privileged functions—the ideological function—takes on particular importance. At first performed by the priests, only much later do ever more specialized intellectuals—poets, philosophers, scientists, writers—take it over. Before going into the concept of ideology, we may just call attention to the social underpinnings of all ideology in a group of specialists who elaborate ideas and present them to the larger society.

d. We must distinguish between activities concerned with physical nature and activities concerned with human beings. The latter arise out of the division of labor, and yet the term "labor" does not quite apply to them. We speak of religious, political, and cultural *functions* rather than of religious, political, or cultural *work*. Let us designate the two groups of activities by the terms *poiesis* and praxis, respectively. *Poiesis* gives human form to the sensuous; it includes man's relations with nature—his labors as a farmer, craftsman, and artist —and more generally, the appropriation of nature by human beings, both of the nature external to themselves and that which is internal to themselves. Praxis comprises interhuman relationships, managerial activities, and the functions of the state as they come into being. In a broad sense, praxis subsumes *poiesis;* in the strict sense, it only designates the *pragmata,* the matters actually deliberated by the members of society.

The distinction proposed here follows the developmental sequence of language viewed as the embodiment of society's consciousness. It emphasizes the way human activities, within the unity of the social, are themselves divided against themselves, constitute a duality.

Poiesis, result of a division in the body social, is in turn divided. Productive labor (agriculture, crafts, and later industry) is devalued in relation to creative activity proper or, more accurately, the activity that is alone regarded as creative, namely, that which an individual pursues in producing a work. The thing, the product, the work come to be distinguished from one another. Similarly in praxis (in the strict sense), some activities come to enjoy specially privileged status: namely, the mediations or activities of intermediaries—the trader, the orator, the political leader.

In the course of this vast process, work comes to be in conflict with itself. It is at once individual and social, differentiated and total, qualitative and quantitative, simple and complex, productive and unproductive, heterogeneous and homogeneous. It comes into conflict with nonwork (idleness, leisure). Work *qua* dialectical process and *qua* content gives rise to a specific form, the form assumed by the product of physical labor: the commodity.

The fact is, praxis is first and foremost *act,* dialectical relation between man and nature, consciousness and things (which can never be legitimately separated, in the manner of philosophers who make them two distinct substances). But if thereby every praxis is content, this content creates forms; it is content only by virtue of the form born of its contradictions; these it usually resolves imperfectly, and seeks to impose coherence on the content. Thus every society is creative of forms. As for the development of praxis, through many vicissitudes and dramas (among them the disappearance of many societies, including the noblest and happiest) it has perpetuated and perfected certain forms. We may mention the forms of politeness, of direct personal relations; the aesthetic forms; formal logic (derived from reflection on discourse); law (rules governing contracts and exchanges); lastly, the commodity (form assumed by the product in the course of the generalizing of exchanges) with its consequence, or rather implication, money. The commodity form has one very important characteristic: it does not detach itself from its content, the labor that has gone into it. As a thing, it is both a use value and an exchange value: a human product. In relation to labor and the inner contradictions of productive labor, the commodity is at once measure and what is measured. It has value only through the labor (the average time of social labor, says Marx) embodied in it, but labor in turn ends up by having value only in so far as it produces commodities and itself becomes a commodity (*qua* time spent on labor). Once launched upon its career, the commodity carries to the end the potentialities inherent in this form. With the commodity, ever greater importance is assumed in praxis by the mediator between the various types of productive labor: the trader. By the latter's activity labor is subjugated and brought into subjection: money becomes primordial, and the intermediaries become more essential than creative or productive activities.

In the first hundred pages of *Capital* Marx shows how a thing, a product assumes, under certain conditions, the form of a commodity. The thing splits in two: without losing its material reality and use value, it is transmuted into an exchange value. The thing as such is subjected to a transubstantiation, whereby it passes from qualitative to quantitative status, from its separate identity to confrontation with other things, from a substantial reality to a pure form (coins, money). The form attains its perfection when every single commodity can be evaluated by one universal equivalent: money.

This analysis of use value and account of its formal development are well known. To Marx, the commodity form, which he traces through each successive transformation, possesses the peculiar capacity of concealing its own essence and origin from the human beings who live with it and by it. The form is fetishized. It appears to be a thing endowed with boundless powers. The form reacts upon its own content and takes possession of it. The thing turns man into *its* thing, disguising its own origins and the secret of its birth, namely, that it is the product of specific human interrelations. This fetishist character of commodities, money, capital, has far-reaching consequences. It generates real appearances that befog "reality" (praxis) the more effectively because they are part of it. Analysis must dispel this fog, cut through the veil of appearance. The fetishized form takes on these two properties: as abstract thing, it becomes autonomous, and dissimulates the real relationships. We shall be coming back to this analysis in closer detail.

"Man's reflections on the forms of social life, and consequently, also, his scientific analysis of these forms, take a course directly opposite to that of their actual historical development. He begins, *post festum*, with the results of the process of development ready to hand before him. The characters that stamp products as commodities, and whose establishment is a necessary preliminary to the circulation of commodities, have already taken on the stability of natural, self-understood forms of social life, before man sets out to decipher—not their historical character, for in his eyes they are immutable —but their meaning."[14]

In other words, the form is deceptive. It induces false impressions, erroneous thinking: namely, the impression of fixity, confusion between the natural (immobile) thing, and the social thing (abstract, hence formed historically). And it carries the whole of society with it in a very special process: reification.

However, these very important observations by Marx are not to be systematized as a single theory of reification, which according to some constitutes the essence of *Capital* and of Marxism generally. The school of Lukács has overestimated the theory of reification to the point of making it the foundation of a philosophy and sociology (the two are regarded as identical in this systematization). Now, the abstract thing, the form (commodity, money, capital) cannot carry the process of reification ("thingification") to its conclusion. It cannot free itself from the human relationships it tends to dominate, to distort, to change into relations between things. It cannot fully exist *qua* thing. It remains an abstract thing for and through active human beings. What it involves is thus an order of formal human interrelations.

"Commodities cannot go to market . . . under their own power. . . . In order that these objects may enter into relations with each other as commodities, their guardians must place themselves in relation to one another, as persons whose will resides in these objects. . . . They must . . . recognize in each other the right of private proprietors. This juridical relation, which expresses itself in the contract, whether such contract be part of a developed legal system or not, is a relationship between two wills, and is but the reflection of the real economic relation between the two."[15]

The abstract thing or form-thing thus involves a formal order of human relationships, namely, contractual relations. The form splits in two: on the one hand, we get the commodity with its social and economic consequences, on the other, the contract with its social and juridical implications. The correspondence between these two aspects is secured by the unity of the underlying process.

The economic study of the process of exchange is matched by another study, that of juridical relations and their consequences. Once the way has been cleared for money and the commodity, once their rule emerges in history, the code of contractual interhuman relations is promulgated: Napoleon's Civil Code, for example. Once such a code has been formally elaborated, it provides a key to the new society, makes it possible to decode bourgeois society and discover the as yet obscure sense it makes.[16]

It must not be forgotten that, underneath the formal appearances, the content persists: work and its dialectical movement (individual and social, qualitative and quantitative, simple and complex work). The theory of the value form refers to the study and theory of division of labor:

"The world of commodities implies the existence of a highly developed division of labor; this division is manifested directly in the great variety of use values, which confront each other as particular commodities and which embody as many different kinds of labor. The division of labor, embracing all the particular kinds of productive occupations, is the complete expression of social labor in its material aspect viewed as labor creating use values. But from the standpoint of commodities and within the process of exchange, it exists only in its results, in the variety of the commodities themselves."[17]

e. The specific character of art and culture would seem to prove that man's appropriation of his own nature (nature within man—sensations and sensibility, needs and desires) falls under the heading of *poiesis* rather than praxis (in the strict sense). It is the works that appropriate man's nature in a given culture. This thesis, however, is not to be formulated or accepted without reservations. The appropriation results from both activities, from their unity that persists even after their separation. We must distinguish between domination over nature (external nature) and appropriation of nature (within man). Control can be exercised over nature without advance in its appropriation. Some societies have stressed appropriation (historic example: Greece), others have stressed control over nature and domination by men of men (historic example: Rome). The respective elements of various societies, cultures, civilizations have differed greatly on this score.

We have also to distinguish between the controlled (dominated or appropriated) sector, and the noncontrolled sector. The latter does not fall entirely within physical nature. Within man, too, there is an area man does not know and does not control, in the individual heart no less than in public, collective history. That one part of human reality, the historical and social, should be known and dominated or appropriated, while another part should be unknown and should continue to operate blindly, is a social and historical fact of major importance. Men make their society and their history, but without knowing how, in a fashion characterized by the ambivalent mixture of knowledge and ignorance, conscious action and blind compulsion.[18]

The two sectors coexist, but theirs is anything but a peaceful coexistence. It is marked by bitter struggles, continually renewed.

Since Marx was familiar with Greek thought,[19] we might assume that he was familiar with the well-known distinction between causes and reasons: determinisms, contingencies and accidents, human will and human choices. These three orders confront and conflict with one another in the life of actual societies. The third order tends to expand and encroach upon the two others, without ever absorbing or eliminating them.

One widely recognized schema distinguishes various levels of praxis: the base or foundation (productive forces: techniques, organization of labor); structures (production and property relations); superstructures (institutions, ideologies). This schema is in keeping with some of the texts by Marx. Does it cover the whole of praxis? Must we look upon it as necessary and sufficient? We do not think so. The same goes for the no less popularized scheme according to which economic life is looked upon as the anatomy of society, and sociology as its physiology. Such schemata freeze into dogmas and become fallacious. They leave out of account the mediations, the encroachments, the interactions, and above all the forms. For instance, in the first of the above-mentioned schemata, what place are we to assign to knowledge? It is closely related to techniques (hence to the "base"), and to ideologies (hence to the "superstructures"). And where do language, logic, and law belong? Both schemata tend to underestimate the importance of human activity, the living (and two-sided) relations between men and their works. They leave out fundamental dialectical "moments," both those relating to need and those relating to work. In short they overlook or break down the concept of praxis.

Without rejecting analysis according to levels, we shall propose another schema that we believe to be faithful to Marx's inspiration. There are three levels of praxis: the repetitive, the innovating, and between these two extremes, the mimetic. In repetitive praxis, the same gestures, the same acts, are performed again and again, within determined cycles. Mimetic praxis follows models; occasionally it creates without imitating—i.e., creates without knowing how or why—but more often imitates without creating.[20] As for inventive, creative praxis, its highest level is reached in revolutionary activity. This activity can be exercised in knowledge and culture (ideology) as well as in the field of politics. Political action, however, concentrates and condenses all partial changes in a total phenomenon—in a revolution that transforms the mode of production, production and property relations, ideas and institutions, the entire way of life. Revolutionary praxis introduces discontinuities into the overall socio-historical process.

This process actually has two aspects: a quantitative aspect and a qualitative one. Technique, knowledge, physical production, the productive forces generally, exhibit a certain continuity as they gradually increase. The qualitative development of society—particularly in the West—is very dramatic in character. It is marked by regression and periods of stagnation. It launches into social existence a seemingly inexhaustible variety of ideas and forms. In the course of this development, radical transformations, historic leaps forward occur. Revolutions put in question society as a whole, with its established forms and orders which no longer express the steadily growing productive forces. Revolutions and comparable mutations disclose societies as totalities: thus, in the course of its transformations, feudalism gradually came to manifest itself as a whole, as a "system." The same has been true of competitive capitalism in more recent times.

Consequently it is correct to say that revolutionary praxis is what introduces concrete (dialectical) intelligibility into social relations. Thanks to it, thought and feeling are once again brought into accord with reality, institutions into accord with the productive forces (the base), social forms into accord with their contents. Here again we encounter the fundamental idea of going beyond a given historical stage, of progressing to a higher stage. It creates intelligibility as living reason in the heads of men and as rationality in social relations.

Revolutionary praxis, born of growth and launched into the historical development, invariably runs headlong into an opposed, conservative political praxis. The latter seeks to preserve established forms, institutions, orders. It tries to hold on to them either by readjusting them to contents which have changed in the process of growth or by denying that any change in content has occurred. Such efforts may be more or less successful, according to the political strength of the various groups, classes, individuals involved. Radical changes are always historically determined, and they may be carried out in two ways: starting from the bottom of society, by revolutionizing praxis as a whole; or starting from the top, by authoritarian acts on the part of institutions, established forms, political leaders (example: Bismarckism in Germany after the failure of the 1848 revolution). Only changes of the first kind are decisive, for only they get rid of obsolete forms. Changes of the second kind are not as far-reaching, but according to Marx they pave the way for more radical transformations.

Here we are faced with another fundamental idea. Everything in society is act, the essence of the human is what it accomplishes. Even the working out of historical necessity involves recourse to action—praxis—if the transition from the possible to the real is to be effected, and so leaves room for human initiative. Every possibility presents mankind with two alternatives—that of greater alienation, that of disalienation. Alienation, like any other process, tends to become real. Disalienation is brought about by conscious struggle—progressively more conscious once the working class appears on the stage of history—against alienation. Everywhere and always social man is inventive, creative; everywhere and always he is in thrall to his own achievements.

Praxis in its supreme realization (creative, revolutionary praxis) does not exclude the theory it animates and verifies. It comprises theoretical decision as well as the decision to act. It involves tactics and strategy.

There is no activity without an aim in view, no act without a program, no political praxis save as the possible, the future, are envisaged.

The concept of praxis and actual praxis should by now begin to reveal the wealth of determinations they contain. We must not be misled by the Hegelian term "determination." Though it is determined, praxis remains open: it always points to the domain of possibility. Dialectically, this is precisely what determination is: the negative that contains the positive, negates the past in the name of the possible, and so manifests it as totality. Every praxis has two historical co-ordinates: one denotes the past, that which has been accomplished, the other the future onto which praxis opens and which it will create. Determination does not signify determinism. Confusion on just this point lies at the bottom of a good many misunderstandings of Marxian thought. Determinisms are inherited from the past; they are forms, systems, structures that somehow survive more or less intact and have yet to be superseded or have as yet been only incompletely superseded: they continue to exert an active influence upon the present. Determinisms do not rule out accident, contingency, or creative efforts on the part of individuals and groups to do away with such survivals.

In examining how praxis (both the reality and the concept) unfolds, we started from the biological—the needs of man as a living being. We briefly surveyed the development of human needs and the levels of reality at which they manifest themselves—anthropological, historical, economic, sociological. We have noted some of the major forms generated in the course of this process.

Is it possible to specify which of the concepts formulated by Marx and Marxism bear upon the special science of sociology, as it has been constituted since Marx's day?

This is possible, at least viewing these concepts as hypotheses. The Marxian sociologist will study the emergence of forms, the way forms react on contents, structures on processes. The results of the processes of change illumine the latter retrospectively on the one hand, and modify them on the other. While any form, once constituted, exhausts the possibilities inherent in it (which are always determined, hence limited), other forms, structures, and systems make their appearance. These "entities" born of change seek to survive, and act upon one another, in society as well as in nature. It is incumbent on the sociologist to analyze and expound all these interactions; the historian studies specific processes (hence the genesis of forms and the formation of structures), and the economist specific forms or structures taken in themselves. The interaction of forms and structures leads them to their end. Therefore the sociologist will study stable, balanced structures with reference to the elements that undermine them: he will study the established "entities" with reference to their ephemeral aspects, that is, dialectically. Study of praxis (including the aspect of it we have named *poiesis*), i.e., of any particular content, leads to a sociology of *forms*, in our view, and does so through a dialectical reversal inherent in the method.

Thus we assign a specific domain to Marxist sociology. Another way of dealing with the question, confining ourselves to the elements in Marx which remain sociologically interesting today, would not get beyond an academic, scholastic framework. Marx the sociologist helps us determine the perspectives of a Marxian sociology.

Such a sociology would accentuate the critical aspect of Marxian thought. The structures generated by the process, the forms created by the contents, tend to immobilize the latter. Radical criticism of structures and forms is thus inherent in knowledge, not just the imposition of a value judgment upon sociology (as a value judgment may be imposed on a statement of fact). The results of praxis alienate human beings, not because they "objectify" human capacities, but because they immobilize creative powers and impede progress to a higher stage. Consequently the concept of alienation does not lose its original force, dwindling to a vague designation of the relations between man and his works, but becomes an integral part of a sociology of structures and forms, of the disintegration of forms and the dissolution of structures.

One last observation on praxis. "Thought and Being are distinct, but at the same time they form a unity," Marx, inspired by Parmenides, wrote in *Manuscripts of 1844*. According to him, philosophy could not restore the unity of thought and being, because it took its point of departure in their difference and stayed within the difference. "The solution of theoretical riddles is a practical task." True praxis is the condition of a real theory. The only true praxis is the revolutionary praxis, which goes beyond the repetitive and the mimetic varieties. "The resolution of theoretical antitheses is possible only in a practical way, by virtue of man's practical energy." Their resolution is by no means a purely conceptual task, but a vital real task which philosophy could not perform precisely because philosophy conceived of it as a purely theoretical task. These philosophical antinomies include subjectivism *vs.* objectivism, spiritualism *vs.* materialism, activity *vs.* passivity (taken abstractly).[21]

Marx's thesis that philosophy must be transcended thus takes on a deeper meaning. Through praxis thought is re-united with being, consciousness with sensuous or physical nature, the mind with spontaneity. Our emphasis upon praxis sanctions neither the pragmatist interpretation, nor the elaboration of a new philosophy, not even a philosophy of praxis. It calls for the analytical study and exposition of praxis itself. This thesis does not relegate philosophy to "the dustbin of history," but situates it in the dialectical movement of consciousness and being, forms and contents. Philosophy was a form distinct (too distinct, too detached) from contents in the course of human development. This development is not thereby endowed with some ontologically specially privileged status, such as would promulgate historical time as explaining man in terms of causality or finality. "Man" retains an ontological foundation. Where? In "nature." Anthropology has a domain of its own, and man can be defined as *sapiens, faber, ludens,* etc. Such definition never justifies separating man from his material foundation, or dissociating culture from nature, or what is acquired from what is spontaneously given. Like the other sciences, sociology carves out a halfway house somewhere between nothingness and the whole of reality. It has no right to set itself up as a total science, claiming to encompass the totality of praxis.[22]

3

Ideology and the
Sociology of Knowledge

The concept of ideology is one of the most original and most comprehensive concepts Marx introduced. It is also one of the most complex and most obscure, though the term is widely employed today. To clarify it, we shall begin with a few preliminary considerations.

a. It is well known that the term "ideology" originated with a philosophical school (empiricist and sensationalist, with a tendency to materialism) which enjoyed considerable influence in France at the close of the eighteenth and the beginning of the nineteenth century. According to the philosophers of this school (Destutt de Tracy is the best known), there is a science of ideas, i.e., of abstract concepts, which studies their genesis and can reconstruct it in full starting from sensations (a conception that goes back to Condillac). This science was called "ideology," and the philosophers who practiced it called themselves "ideologists" (*idéologues*).

Marx transformed the meaning of the term—or, more accurately, he and Engels gave their approval to a transformation in meaning which the term underwent once the school of the *idéologues* died out. The term now became a pejorative one. Instead of denoting a theory, it came to denote a phenomenon the theory accounted for. This phenomenon now took on entirely different dimensions. As interpreted by the French ideologists, ideology was limited to accounting for individual representations by a causal psychology. To Marx and Engels, the phenomenon under study became a collection of representations characteristic of a given epoch and society. For example: *The German Ideology*. The original meaning was not entirely lost sight of: Marx aimed at formulating a theory of general, i.e., social representations; he defined the elements of an explanatory genesis of "ideologies" and related the latter to their historical and sociological conditions.

b. If we introduce terms such as "opacity" and "transparency" (of a given society) in our exposition, we may be charged with substituting images for scientific definitions. However, Marx himself uses such "images" and views them as elements of knowledge. "Transparency" stands for "immediate presence or intelligibility"—a quality that is not often found in "representations."

"Since Robinson Crusoe's experiences are a favorite theme with political economists, let us take a look at him on his island. Moderate though he be, yet some few wants he has to satisfy, and must therefore do a little useful work of various sorts, such as making tools and furniture, taming goats, fishing and hunting. Of his prayers and the like we take no account, since they are a source of pleasure to him, and he looks upon them as so much recreation. . . . All the relations between Robinson Crusoe and the objects that form this wealth of his own creation, are . . . simple and transparent. . . .

"Let us now transport ourselves from Robinson's island bathed in light to the European Middle Ages shrouded in darkness. . . . For the very reason that personal dependency forms the foundation of society,[23] there is no necessity for labor and its products to assume a form different from their reality. They take the shape . . . of services in kind and payments in kind. Here the particular and natural form of labor—and not as in a society based on production of commodities, its general abstract form—is the immediate social form of labor. . . . In the patriarchal industries of a peasant family that produces corn, cattle, yarn, linen, and clothing for home use, these different articles are, as regards the family, so many products of its labor, but as between themselves, they are not commodities. . . .

"Let us now picture to ourselves . . . a community of free individuals, carrying on their work with the means of production in common, in which the labor power of all the different individuals is consciously applied as the combined labor of the community. . . . The social relations of the individual producers, with regard both to their labor and to its products, are in this case perfectly simple and transparent, and that with regard not only to production but also to distribution. . . .

"Trading nations properly so-called exist only in the Intermundia of the ancient world, like the gods of Epicurus or like Jews in the pores of Polish society. Those ancient social organisms of production are, as compared with bourgeois society, extremely simple and transparent. But they are founded either on the immature development of man individually, who has not yet severed the umbilical cord that unites him with his fellow men in a primitive tribal community, or upon direct relations of subjection. . . .

"The life-process of society which is based on the process of material production does not strip off its mystical veil until it is treated as production by freely associated men and is consciously regulated by them in accordance with a settled plan. . . ."[24]

Clearly, according to Marx, the social consciousness generated by a given praxis faithfully reflects it only in specific situations: namely, when the praxis is not shrouded in mystical veils, when interhuman relations are direct, without "opaque" intermediaries. The various types of social praxis within specific social structures and modes of production give rise to "representations." These representations increase or decrease the degree of a given society's "opacity." They illumine or obscure the society. Sometimes they illumine it with a false clarity and sometimes they plunge it into shadow or darkness in the name of a doctrine even obscurer than the reality generating it. Social reality, i.e. interacting human individuals and groups, produces *appearances* which are something more and else than mere illusions. Such appearances are the modes in which human activities manifest themselves within the whole they constitute at any given moment—call them modalities of consciousness. They have far greater consistency, let alone coherence, than mere illusions or ordinary lies. Appearances have reality, and reality involves appearances. In particular, the production of commodities is enveloped in a fog. We have to keep getting back to the commodity, for here we find the key to Marxian thought and sociology. In analytical reflection, the commodity is a pure form, hence something transparent. In practical everyday experience, on the other hand, it is opaque and a cause of opaqueness. The very existence of the commodity is strange, the more so because men are not aware of its strangeness.

"A commodity appears, at first sight, a very trivial thing, and easily understood. Analysis shows that it is in reality a very peculiar thing, abounding in metaphysical subtleties and theological niceties."[25]

It has a "mystical character"; it exists only thanks to human beings in their interrelations, and yet it exists apart from them and modifies their relations, reifying the latter and making them abstract. Many centuries had to go by before critical thought would unmask this fetishism, revealing its mystery as the power of money and capital. Thus the commodity, as a form and a system implying the existence of money and capital, must inevitably give rise to an opaque society. In popular terms, the opaqueness is expressed in the fact that money holds sway over human beings: people with money intrigue their way to power, the powers-that-be constitute an occult order. The opaqueness or nontransparency of society is thus a social, or rather, a socio-economic fact. Only revolutionary praxis by articulating the (true) theory and furthering (practical, verifying) modes of action restores the conditions for transparency. Revolutionary praxis does away with the conditions illusory representations thrive on, brings about new conditions to dispel them.

This much is clear. However, Marx's writings contain two definitions of ideology sufficiently different to raise questions and call for an elucidation of the concept.

Ideology, we are told, is an inverted, truncated, distorted reflection of reality. In ideologies men and their conditions appear upside down like images on the lens of a camera; supposedly, this comes about as the result of a specific biological process, similar to the physical process which accounts for the way images are reversed on the retina. In their representations, individuals similarly grasp their own reality "upside down," and this fact is part of reality. Consciousness is no more or less than individual consciousness, yet one law of consciousness decrees that it must be perceived as a thing apart from the self. Human beings do not perceive themselves exactly as they are, but instead as projected upon a screen. Illusory representations of reality—the illusionism being ordained by this reality—refer either to nature and man's relations with nature or to interhuman relations. Ideologies, by this account, come down to false representations of history or to abstractions from history. Every ideology, then, is a collection of errors, illusions, mystifications, which can be accounted for by reference to the historical reality it distorts and transposes.[26]

Study of ideologies thus leads to a critical view of history. General representations (philosophy, law, religion, art, knowledge itself)—cloudy precipitations rising from human brains—are superpositions over material and biological processes which can be empirically observed without them. Morals, religion, metaphysics, and the other aspects of ideology, and the corresponding forms of consciousness are only seemingly autonomous. "They have no history, no development," i.e., they cannot be understood unless they are related to the modes of production and exchange obtaining in a given society at a given moment. "It is not consciousness that determines life, but life that determines consciousness," according to the famous formula, so often quoted out of context. Actually, the context is very clear: it says that there are only two ways to understand history. Either we start from consciousness; in which case we fail to account for real life. Or we start from real life; then we come up against this ideological consciousness that has no reality, and must account for it. Historical materialism puts an end to the speculation which starts from consciousness, from representations, and hence from illusions: "Where speculation on real life stops, real and positive science begins. The object of such science is practical activity, the process of human development on the practical plane."

This process is self-sufficient. Reality and rationality are inherent in it. Knowledge puts an end to phraseology, to ideology. More particularly, when philosophy devotes itself to representation of reality, it loses its medium of existence. What takes the place of philosophy? Study of the results of historical development, which have no interest, no meaning, no value outside history. Inherited philosophical concepts can serve merely to facilitate the ordering of the historical materials, indicate the sequence of successive deposits.

What follows in the same work (*The German Ideology*) goes far to correct what is extremist in this theory. Once ideology is related to the real conditions that gave rise to it, it ceases to be completely illusory, entirely false. For what is ideology? Either it is a theory that is unconscious of its own presuppositions, its basis in reality, and true meaning, a theory unrelated to action, i.e., without consequences or with consequences different from those expected and foreseen. Or it is a theory that generalizes special interests—class interests—by such means as abstraction, incomplete or distorted representations, appeals to fetishism.

If so, it is erroneous to maintain that every ideology is pure illusion. It appears that ideology is not, after all, to be accounted for by a sort of ontological fate that compels consciousness to differ from being. Ideologies have truly historical and sociological foundations, in the division of labor on the one hand, in language on the other.

Man possesses consciousness; on this score the philosophers who formulated and elucidated the concept of consciousness were right. Where the philosophers went astray was when they isolated consciousness from the conditions and objects of consciousness, from it diverse and contradictory relations with all that is not consciousness, when they conceived of consciousness as "pure," but above all when they ascribed "purity" to the historically earliest forms of consciousness. In this way they raised insoluble speculative problems. For from the outset the supposed purity of consciousness is tainted with original sin. It cannot escape the curse of "being soiled with a matter that here takes the form of agitated layers of air, in short, language." Language is as old as consciousness. There is no consciousness without language, for language is the real, practical consciousness, which exists for other human beings, and hence for beings that have become conscious. Marx discovers that language is not merely the instrument of a pre-existing consciousness. It is at once the natural and the social medium of consciousness, its mode of existence. It comes into being with the need for communication, with human intercourse in the broadest sense. Consequently, being inseparable from language, consciousness is a social creation.

It remains to note what human beings communicate to one another, what they have to say. To begin with, the objects of their communications include the sensorily perceived environment and their immediate ties with other human beings. They also refer to nature in so far as it is a hostile power before which man feels helpless. Human consciousness begins with an animal, sensuous awareness of nature, though even at this stage it is already social. This gives rise to a first misrepresentation: a religion of nature which mistakes *social* relations (however elementary) for *natural* relations, and vice versa. What we might call "tribal consciousness" emerges out of earlier barbarism, earlier illusions, as productivity expands, as tools are perfected, and as needs and population increase. What had hitherto been a purely biological division of labor (based on sex, age, physical strength, etc.) begins to become a technological and social division of labor. As the society develops, it takes on ever new forms and subdivisions (city *vs.* countryside, social *vs.* political functions, trade *vs.* production—not to mention the ever sharper distinction that comes to be drawn between individual and social labor, partial and over-all labor, etc.). So far as the development of ideologies is concerned, the most important division is that between physical and intellectual labor, between creative action (operations upon things with the aid of tools and machines) and action on human beings by means of non-material instruments, the primary and most important of which is language. *From this point forward, consciousness becomes capable of detachment from reality*, may now begin to construct abstractions, to create a "pure theory." Theology supplants the religion of nature, philosophy supplants religion, morality supplants traditional manners and customs, etc. Ever more elaborate representations are built up, and overlay the direct, immediate consciousness, now felt to be at once crude and deluded, for having remained at the natural, sensorial level. When these abstract representations come into conflict with reality, i.e., with existing social relations, the social relations themselves have become contradictory, both as between themselves and between them and their social base—namely, the productive forces (the technological division and the social organization of labor).

These representations give rise to theories. Consequently, what we are dealing with is not detached, isolated representations, but ideas given coherent form by "ideologists," a new kind of specialist. Those who wield material (economic and political) power within the established social and juridical order also wield "spiritual" power. The representations, i.e., the consciousness of society, are elaborated into a systematic idealizing of existing conditions, those conditions that make possible the economic, social, and political primacy of a given group or class. Individuals active on the plane of praxis play an important part in forming the general consciousness and in excluding representations contrary to the interest of the ruling groups. As a result, "their ideas are the dominant ideas of their epoch," but in a way which leaves room for invention. For instance, when the king, the nobility, and the bourgeoisie are striving with one another for dominance, we find a political theory of the separation of powers. To understand a given ideology, we have to take into account everything that is going on in the higher circles of the society in question—classes, fractions of classes, institutions, power struggles, diverging and converging interests. It must also be kept in mind that the "ideologists" themselves are rarely active as members of their given class or group. This detachment on their part is passed on in their "treatments" of the realities they represent, whether in justification or condemnation. The theoretical conflicts are not unrelated to the actual conflicts discussed, but the verbalizations do not accurately, point by point, reflect the realities they represent. This leaves room for revolutionary ideas when a revolutionary group or class actually exists in the society, with a practical end in view: namely, the transformation of society through solving its problems, resolving existing contradictions.

According to Marx (and Engels), ideologies possess the following characteristics:

1 Their starting point is reality, but a fragmentary, partial reality; in its totality it escapes the ideological consciousness because the conditions of this consciousness are limited and limiting, and the historical process eludes the human will under such conditions of intervention.

2 They refract (rather than reflect) reality *via* preexisting representations, selected by the dominant groups and acceptable to them. Old problems, old points of view, old vocabularies, traditional modes of expression thus come to stand in the way of the new elements in society and new approaches to its problems.

3 Ideological representations, though distorted and distorting not because of some mysterious fate but as a result of the historical process within which they become a factor, tend to constitute a self-sufficient whole

and lay claim to be such. The whole, however, comprises praxis, and it is precisely this that ideologies distort by constructing an abstract, unreal, fictitious theory of the whole. The degrees of reality and unreality in any ideology vary with the historical era, the class relations, and other conditions obtaining at a given moment. Ideologies operate by extrapolating the reality they interpret and transpose. They culminate in systems (theoretical, philosophical, political, juridical), all of which are characterized by the fact that they lay behind the actual movement of history. At the same time it must be admitted that every ideology worthy of the name is characterized by a certain breadth and a real effort at rationality. One typical example studied by Marx and Engels is German philosophy between the end of the eighteenth and the middle of the nineteenth century. Every great ideology strives to achieve universality. The claim to universality is unjustified, however, save when the ideology represents a revolutionary class during the time it serves as the vehicle of historical interests and goals with genuinely universal significance. This was the case with the middle classes in the period of their rise to power.

4 Consequently, ideologies have two aspects. On the one hand, they are general, speculative, abstract; on the other, they are representative of determinate, limited, special interests. In setting out to answer all questions, all problems, they create a comprehensive view of the world. At the same time they reinforce specific ways of life, behavior patterns, "values" (if we may use here a terminology that does not occur in Marx's writings).

Ideologies are thus ignorant of the exact nature of their relations with praxis—do not really understand their own conditions and presuppositions, nor the actual consequences to which they are leading. Ignorant of the implications of their own theories, they comprehend neither the causes of which they are effects, nor the effects which they are actually causing; the real why and how escapes them. At the same time they are inescapably involved in praxis. They are at once starting points and results of action in the world (however effective or ineffectual). Ideological representations invariably serve as instruments in the struggles between groups (peoples, nations) and classes (and fractions of classes). But their intervention in such struggles takes the form of masking the true interests and aspirations of the groups involved, universalizing the particular and mistaking the part for the whole.

5 Since they have a starting point and a foothold in reality (in praxis), or rather to the extent that they do, ideologies are not altogether false. According to Marx, we have to distinguish among ideology, illusion, and lies, on the one hand, and ideology, myths, and utopias on the other hand. Ideologies may contain class illusions, have recourse to outright lying in political struggles and yet be related to myths and utopias. Historically, all sorts of illusory, deceptive representations have been inextricably mixed up in ideological thinking with real concepts —i.e. scientific insights. Sometimes the ideology has served as the vehicle of sound thinking, sometimes as agent of its distortion or supression. The evaluation of ideological thinking can only be done *post facto*, patiently, with the aid of some more or less radical critical thought. The typical example cited by Marx and Engels is German philosophy. Thanks to Germany's economic and social backwardness, its thinkers were capable of speculative thought in the first half of the nineteenth

century, whereas in the same period English thinkers were creating theories of political economy (the theory of competitive capitalism) and the French were operating on the plane of direct political action (making revolutions). The Germans transposed praxis to the realm of metaphysics. In their systems it is so heavily disguised as to be all but unrecognizable. This was perfectly in keeping with the actual prospects of their nation, which were at once limitless (in the abstract) and severely limited (practically speaking). At the same time, however, they did give expression to some new concepts—among others, the concept of dialectical change—which were eventually integrated in scientific theory and revolutionary praxis. It is incumbent on critical thought and revolutionary action to salvage what is valid from the wreckage of collapsing systems and crumbling ideologies.

6 Thus it may be said that ideologies make room for nonscientific abstractions, whereas concepts are scientific abstractions (for instance, the concepts of use value and of the commodity). Such concepts do not remain forever shrouded in the mists of abstraction; as we have seen, they are integrated in praxis, though we still have to specify just how. They enter into praxis in two ways: as a constraining factor, and as a form of persuasion. Abstract ideas have no power in themselves, but people who hold power (economic or political) make use of representations in order to justify their actions. Moreover, and this is the main point, the most completely elaborated ideological representations find their way into language, become a permanent part of it. They supply vocabularies, formulations, turns of thought which are also turns of phrase. Social consciousness, awareness of how multifarious and contradictory social action can

be, changes only in this way: by acquiring new terms and idioms to supplant obsolete linguistic structures. Thus it is not language that generates what people say. Language does not possess this magical power or possesses it only fitfully and dubiously. What people say derives from praxis—from the performance of tasks, from the division of labor—arises out of real actions, real struggles in the world. What they actually do, however, enters consciousness only by way of language, by being said. Ideologies mediate between praxis and consciousness (i.e., language). This mediation can also serve as a screen, as a barrier, as a brake on consciousness. Consider the words, symbols, expressions that religions have created. Revolutionary theory, too, has created its own language and introduced it into the social consciousness; the most favorable conditions for this occur when a rising class is mature enough to take in new terms and assimilate new concepts. Even then we must expect to run into formidable obstacles. These are created not only by voluntary actions of contemporaries, but also by long-accepted ideas reflecting contemporaries' limited horizons. An individual member of the middle class is not necessarily malicious or stupid, but he is incapable of rising above the mental horizon of his class. His outlook is formulated in the medium of language, which moreover is the language of society as a whole. Now, language—not only the language of ideologists (e.g., philosophers) but also of all those who speak—distorts practical reality. According to Marx,[27] neither thought nor language forms an autonomous domain. Language, this repository of ideas in the keeping of society as a whole, is full of errors and illusions, trivial truths as well as profound ones. There is always the problem of making the transition from the world of representations (ideas) to the real world, and this problem is none other than that of making the transition from language to life. The problem thus has multiple aspects—the actually existing language, ideologies, praxis, the class situation, the struggles actually going on. When the bourgeois speaks of "human" rights, "human" conditions, etc., he actually means bourgeois conditions, bourgeois rights, etc. He does not distinguish between the two because his very language has been fashioned by the bourgeoisie.[28]

Marx, then, tries to situate language within praxis, in relation to ideologies, classes, and social relationships. Language is important, but is not by itself the crucial factor. Let us go back briefly to the commodity. In one sense, every commodity is a sign: *qua* exchange value it is only the outward and visible sign of the human labor expended to produce it. However, "If it be declared that the social characters assumed by objects, or the material form assumed by the social qualities of labor under the regime of a definite mode of production, are mere signs, it is in the same breath also declared that these characteristics are arbitrary fictions sanctioned by the so-called universal consent of mankind."[29]

This view, according to which every commodity is a sign and which was much in favor during the eighteenth century, is ideological; it is not a conceptual, scientific account of the puzzling forms assumed by social relations.[30] In analyzing language or this other form, the commodity, we must isolate its formal character, but we must never separate it from its other aspects—content, development, history, social relations, praxis.

To gain a better understanding of the Marxian concept of ideology, we may compare it with the "collective representations" of the Durkheim school. In a way, every ideology is a "collective representation," but whereas to Durkheim society is an abstract entity, to Marx it results from practical interactions among groups and individuals. Thus a given ideology does not characterize a society as a whole; it arises out of individual inventions made within the social framework in which groups, whether castes or classes, struggle to assert themselves and gain dominance. On the other hand, ideologies do not affect individual minds from the outside, for they are not extraneous to the real life of individuals. Ideologies utilize *the language of real life*, and hence are not vehicles of the coercive pressure society exerts on the individual (according to Durkheim's sociology). Those who use ideologies rarely hesitate to resort to force when this is justified by the same ideologies, in which case we have brutal constraint exercised by the powers-that-be. Ideologies as such, however, as instruments of persuasion, guide the individual and give him a sense of purpose. Viewed from outside, ideologies seem self-contained, rational systems; viewed from inside, they imply faith, conviction, adherence. In pledging his allegiance to a given ideology the individual believes he is fulfilling himself. In actual fact he does not fulfill himself, he loses himself, he becomes alienated, though this is not immediately apparent to him, and when it does become apparent it is often too late. Thus ideologies impose certain obligations on individuals, but these obligations are voluntarily accepted. The inner or outer penalties imposed by ideologies are expected, demanded by the individuals concerned. Thus the power of ideologies is very different from that of Durkheim's "collective representations."

Every society, every authority has to be accepted. A

given social structure, with its specific social and juridical relations, must obtain the consensus of a majority, if not the totality of its members. No social group, no constituted society is possible without such adherence, and sociologists are justified in stressing this consensus. But how is the consensus arrived at? How do conquerors, rulers, masters, those in power make oppression acceptable? Marx and Engels have repeatedly emphasized the fact that no society is based on sheer brute force alone. Every social form finds its rationale in the society's growth and development, in the level its productive forces and social relations have attained. It is the role of ideologies to secure the assent of the oppressed and exploited. Ideologies represent the latter to themselves in such a way as to wrest from them, in addition to material wealth, their "spiritual" acceptance of this situation, even their support. Class ideologies create three images of the class that is struggling for dominance: an image for itself; an image of itself for other classes, which exalts it; an image of itself for other classes, which devalues them in their own eyes, drags them down, tries to defeat them, so to speak, without a shot being fired. Thus the feudal nobility put forward an image of itself—a multiple image with multiple facets: the knight, the nobleman, the lord. Similarly the middle class elaborated an image of itself for its own use: as the bearer of human reason in history, as uniquely endowed with good and honorable intentions, finally as alone possessed with capacity for efficient organization. It also has its own images of the other classes: the good worker, the bad worker, the agitator, the rabble-rouser. Lastly it puts forward a self-image for the use of other classes: how its money serves the general good, promotes human happiness, how the middle-class organization of society promotes population growth and material progress.

No historical situation can ever be stabilized once and for all, though that is what ideologies aim at. Other forms of consciousness and rival ideologies make their appearance and join the fray. Only another ideology or a true theory can struggle against an ideology. No form of consciousness ever constitutes a last, last word, no ideology ever manages to transform itself into a permanent system. Why? Because praxis always looks forward to new possibilities, a future different from the present. The consensus an ideology succeeds in bringing about in its heyday, when it is still growing and militant, eventually crumbles away. It is supplanted by another ideology, one that brings fresh criticism to bear on the existing state of affairs and promises something new.

When we analyze more closely the views on ideology propounded by Marx and Engels, we make out the elements for an orderly outline of its origin and development.

a. First of all, some representations are illusory, for they arise prior to the conditions under which concepts can be formed. Thus, before the concept of historical time had arisen, there were representations concerning the succession of events, how the undertakings of a given society or group and its leaders were initiated and succeeded or failed as they did. Such representations had a mythical, legendary, epical, heroic character. Elaborated by still relatively undifferentiated social groups, they were refined by priests and poets. The same is true of the earliest representations of natural forces and of the few human acts as yet capable of modifying natural processes. Such representations ascribed to human beings, or rather to certain individuals, a fictitious power of control over the unknown, and so accounted for the lesser ability and inability of other men and of society as a whole to do as much.

b. Related to these elaborations are the early cosmogonies and theogonies, images of the world which were often projected against a background of the actual life of social groups, and the actual organization in villages and towns. These great constructions included interpretations of the sexes (masculinity, femininity), of the family (according to division of labor, age), of the elements (often presented in pairs—earth and air, fire and water), of the relationship between leaders and subordinates, of life and death.

Were these grandiose images of society, time and space, a history scarcely begun, the prehistory of the race—were they ideologies? Yes and no. Yes, to the degree they justified the nascent inequalities among men, including possession (primitive appropriation) of a territory by a single group and seizure of the group resources—the scanty surplus product—by its leaders. No, because it is not yet possible to speak at this stage of classes or even of castes. No, because these constructions of the mind are works of art—more like monuments than abstract systems. They belong to the same category as styles in art history, compendia of moral wisdom, "cultures." They show to what extent rulers feel the need to justify themselves in the eyes of the vanquished and the oppressed: such works serve both to justify and to consolidate their rule.

c. It does not seem that in Marx's view mythologies can be regarded as ideologies. They are much closer to genuine poetry than to formal constructions. Marx thought that Greek mythology, the soil that nourished Greek art, was an expression of the real life of the people, an ever fresh source of the "eternal" charm of this art. The Greek myths and the Greek gods were symbols of man or rather of his powers. They gave in magnified form a picture of how human beings appropriate their own nature—in the various activities of their own lives (warfare, metal working), in games, love, and enjoyment.

Cosmogonies, myths, and mythologies are turned into ideologies only when they become ingredients in religion, especially in the great religions that lay claim to universality. Then the images and tales are cut off from the soil that nourished them, the beauty of which they represented to the eye and mind. Now they take on different meaning. The great religions' all-inclusive character and claim to universality are marked on the one hand by abstractness and by loss of their original local flavor, and on the other by an ever growing gap between individuals, between groups, between peoples, and between classes. The great religions were born concomitantly with consolidation of the power of the state, the formation of nations, and the rise of class antagonisms. Religions make use not of a knowledge freed of illusion, but of illusions antedating knowledge. To these they add unmistakably ideological representations, i.e., representations elaborated in order to disguise praxis and to give it a specific direction. As theoretical constructions they alternate between a kind of poetry borrowed from the earlier cosmogonies and sheer mystification intended to justify the acts of the powers-that-be.

Incontestably, according to Marx, religion in general (religion to the extent it lays claim to universality, to representing the fate of mankind, of the human species) is the prototype and model of all ideology. All criticism begins and is renewed again with the criticism of religion. Radical criticism, i.e., criticism that goes to the roots, tirelessly keeps going back to the analysis of religious alienation.

Summing up Marx's thought, we can now formulate the sociological features of any ideology. It deals with a segment of reality, namely, human weakness: death, suffering, helplessness. It includes interpretations of the wretched portion of reality, consciousness of which, if taken in isolation and overemphasized, acts as a brake on all creation, all progress. By virtue of their link with "reality"—a reality transposed and interpreted—ideologies can affect reality by imposing rules and limitations on actually living men. In other words, ideologies can be part of actual experience, even though they are unreal and formal, reflect only a portion of human reality. They offer a way of seeing the world and of living, that is to say, up to a certain point, a praxis which is at once illusory and efficacious, fictitious and real.

Ideologies account for and justify a certain number of actions and situations which need to be accounted for and justified, the more so the wronger and more absurd they are (i.e., in process of being surmounted and superseded). Thus every ideology represents a vision or conception of the world, a *Weltanschauung* based on extrapolations and interpretations.

Another feature of ideologies is their perfectibility. An ideology may encounter problems, but not of a kind to shake it fundamentally. Adjustment is made, details are altered, but the essentials are left intact. This gives rise to passionate and passionately interesting discussions between conservatives and innovators, dogmatists and heretics, champions of the past and champions of the future. As a result, a given ideology becomes associated with a group (or a class, but always a group active within a class: other groups within this class may remain ideologically passive, though they may be most active in other respects). Within the group that takes up the ideology, it serves as pretext for zealousness, sense of common purpose, and then the group tends to become a sect. Adherence to the ideology makes it possible to despise those who do not adhere to it, and, needless to say, leads to their conversion or condemnation. It becomes a pseudo-totality which closes in upon itself the moment it runs into its external or internal boundaries, whether limitations or outside resistances. In short, it becomes a *system*.

Man has emerged from nature in the course of the historical process of production—production of himself and of material goods. Consciousness, as we have seen, emerges at the level of the sensuous, and then rises above it without being cut off from it. This practical relationship, which is essentially and initially based upon labor, is consequently broadened to include the entire praxis of a society in which the various kinds of labor become differentiated and unequal. At this point, objects, situations, actions acquire specific "meanings" in relation to the over-all "meaning" of social life and the course it follows. However, the human groups assigned to perform productive physical labor were unable for many a long century to elaborate a conception adequate to their situation, to the part they actually played in social praxis, which is the essence of their activity. Multiple conflicts are caused by the scarcity of goods, poverty, and bitter struggles over the tiny surplus of wealth produced. In the course of these conflicts, the conditions that made possible production of a surplus, however small, and sometimes production itself, were destroyed. In peace as in war, the interests of the productive groups were sacrificed. On the symbolic plane of ideology, these sacrifices were given an aura of ideality and spirituality. In actual fact, there was nothing mysterious about the sacrifice: the oppressed were sacrificed to the oppressors, and the oppressors to the very conditions of oppression —the gods, the Fates, the goals of their political actions. As a result, products and works acquired a transcendent significance, which amounted to an ideological and symbolic negation of their actual significance. All this served to justify the actions of the ruling groups and classes seeking to control the means of production and lay hands on the surplus product. Man's appropriation of nature took place within the framework of ownership, that is, the privative appropriation of the social surplus by privileged groups, to the exclusion of other groups, whether within the given society or outside it, and so gave rise to endless tension and struggle. Religion expressed this general attitude of the privileged groups and classes, which was broadened into an ideology that held out to other groups and classes the hope either of oppression eventually coming to an end one day or of being allowed to share in the advantages of oppression themselves.

The features we have just stressed in religion (or, more accurately, in religions which have theoretical systems) are also to be found in philosophy, though there are certain differences. The philosophers elaborate the incomplete rationality which is present in social praxis and confusedly expressed in language—the logos. Thus philosophy breaks off in turn from religion, from poetry, from politics, and finally from scientific knowledge, and as against these more or less specialized domains, claims to express totality. But religion, the state, and even art and science make the same claim. The difference is that, whereas the latter merely use the concept of totality for their own purposes, philosophy also refines it. Unlike the other ideological activities, philosophy contains a self-transcending principle. Philosophical systems reflect human aspirations, they aim at rigorous demonstrations, they express symbols of human reality. The systems eventually disintegrate, but the problems they raised, the concepts they formulated, the themes they treated do not disappear. They enter into culture, affect all thought, in short, become part of consciousness. The relationship between philosophy and praxis (including the consciousness of praxis) is thus more complex and far more fruitful than that between religion or the state and the same praxis.

Among the philosophical attempts at totality, i.e., at achieving a system at once closed and encompassing all "existents," the systems of morals are the most ideological in character. They set themselves above praxis, promulgating absolute principles and eternal "ethical" truths. They prescribe sacrifice for the oppressed, promising them compensations. They also prescribe sacrifice for the oppressors, when the conditions of their dominance are threatened. Consequently, every morality is dictated by the ruling class, according to its needs and interests in a given situation; the generality it claims is dubious, its universality illusory. It is not on the moral (ethical) plane that the universal is concretely realized. Morality substitutes fictitious needs and aspirations reflecting the constant pressure of the ruling class for the real needs and aspirations of the oppressed. More particularly, under capitalism human needs diverge sharply into highly refined, abstract needs on the one hand, and crude, grossly simplified needs on the other. This dissociation is sanctioned and consecrated by the bourgeois moralities. The latter go so far as to justify the state of non-having—the situation of man separated from objects and works which are meaningful themselves and give concrete, practical meaning to life.

> "The state of non-having is the extremest form of spiritualism, a state in which man is totally unreal and inhumanity totally real: it is a state of very positive having—the having of hunger, cold, sickness, crime, degradation, stupor, every conceivable inhuman and antinatural thing."[31]

Now, objects, i.e., goods, products, and works of social man, are the foundation of social man's objective being, his being for himself as well as for others. To be deprived of objects is to be deprived of social existence, of human relations with others and with oneself. Morality *qua* ideology masks this privation and even substitutes a fictitious plenitude for it: a sense of righteousness, a mistaken, factitious satisfaction in nonfulfillment of the self.

Political economy (at least in its beginnings) elaborates scientific concepts—social labor, exchange value, distribution of the over-all income, etc. At the same time it contains an ideology. It is a "true moral science," even "the most moral of all the sciences." Its gospel is saving, i.e., abstinence. "The less you are . . . the more you have. . . . All the things you cannot do, your money can do."[32]

Thus scientific concepts are all mixed up with a moralistic ideology, in a way its own authors do not notice. The wheat is separated from the chaff only later, in the name of radical criticism, in connection with revolutionary praxis.

Summing up: as Marx saw it, ideology involves the old problem of error and its relation to the truth. Marx does not formulate this problem in abstract, speculative, philosophical terms, but in concrete historical terms with reference to praxis. Unlike philosophy, the Marxian theory of ideology tries to get back to the origin of representations. It retains one essential philosophical contribution: emergent truth is always mixed up with illusion and error. The theory discards the view that error, illusion, falsity, stand off in sharp and obvious distinction from knowledge, truth, certainty. There is continual two-way dialectical movement between the true and the false, which transcends the historical situation that gave rise to these representations. As Hegel had seen, error and illusion are "moments" of knowledge, out of which the truth emerges. But truth does not reside in the Hegelian "spirit." It does not precede its historical and social conditions, even though it may be anticipated. Thus Hegel's philosophical—i.e., speculative, abstract—theory is transformed into a historical and sociological theory, a continuation of philosophy in the sense that it preserves the latter's universal character.

The representations men form of the world, of society, of groups and individuals, remain illusory as long as the conditions for real representation have not ripened. One notable example is how time was represented—a sense of society, of the city-state, as existing in time—prior to the emergence of fully elaborated concepts of history and historical knowledge. These last are rooted in an active social consciousness of the changes taking place within the praxis. While the mists surrounding natural phenomena are being dispelled, the mystery (the opacity) of social life keeps thickening. While increasing human control over nature (technology, the division of labor) makes it possible to elaborate nonideological concepts of physical nature, the actions of the ruling classes throw a veil of obscurity over social life. Praxis expands in scope, grows more complex and harder to grasp, while consciousness and science play an increasingly effective part in it. Thus it has been possible for illusory representations (mythologies, cosmogonies) to become an integral part of styles and cultures (including Greek culture). They must now give way to knowledge. Revolutionary praxis and Marxism *qua* knowledge do away with the ideologies. According to Marx, Marxism has gone beyond ideology—it signals and hastens the end of ideology. Nor is it a philosophy, for it goes beyond philosophy and translates it into practice. It is not a morality, but a theory of moralities. It is not an aesthetics, but it contains a theory of works of art, of the conditions for their production, how they originate and how they pass away. It discloses—not by some power of "pure" thought but by deeds (the revolutionary praxis)—the conditions under which ideologies and works of man generally, including whole cultures or civilizations, are produced, run their course, and pass away.

It is on the basis of conscious revolutionary praxis that thought and action are articulated dialectically, and that knowledge "reflects" praxis, i.e., is constituted as reflection on praxis. Until then knowledge was characterized precisely by its failure to "reflect" reality, namely, praxis, could only transpose it, distort it, confuse it with illusions—in short, knowledge was ideological.

At the height of its development, ideology becomes a weapon deliberately used in the class struggle. It is a mystifying representation of social reality, or the process of change, of its latent tendencies and its future. At this stage—in contemporary racism, for instance—the "real" element is present; the human species does in fact include varieties and variations, ethnic groups and ethnic differences. But in racism extrapolation and transposition are carried to fantastic lengths; the extrapolation of a real element is combined with "values," and the whole systematized with extreme rigidity. Consequently racist ideology can hardly be mentioned in the same breath with such a philosophy, say, as Kant's. In the twentieth century, ideologizing has reached a sort of apogee within the framework of imperialism, world wars, and a monopolistic capitalism linked with the state. At the same time and because of this, ideology is discredited: extreme ideologizing is accompanied by a certain conviction that "the end of ideology" has been reached. But ideology is not so easily eliminated; to the contrary, it is marked by sudden flare-ups and makes surprising comebacks. Aversion from ideological excess is no more than a pale foretaste of the transparency still to be achieved by revolutionary praxis and its theoretical elaboration on the basis of Marx's work.

In this situation, a sociology inspired by Marxism might well address itself to the relations between the following concepts, which are still insufficiently distinguished: ideology and knowledge, utopia and anticipation of the future, poetry and myth. Such a critical study needs to be taken up again in our changing world. Here is a choice theme for the sociologist, one with plenty of scope both for critical thought and for the most "positive" findings: the distance between ideology and practice, between current representations of reality and the reality itself. . . .

4

Sociology and Social Classes

Capitalism has displayed a vitality and elasticity Marx could not foresee. And yet Marx's predictions, let us not hesitate to keep repeating this, have come true. On the basis of an analysis at once minute and bearing upon the phenomenon as a whole, he predicted the end of competitive capitalism under the combined effect of two forces —the working class on the one hand, the increasing concentration (and centralization) of capital on the other hand. And indeed, because of the continuous, contradictory action of these two forces competitive capitalism did in fact come to an end. These social and political forces did in fact between them destroy the monolithic unity of nineteenth century capitalism and its ruling class, the bourgeoisie. What happened was that the "world"—more accurately, the world market—split into three sectors: monopoly capitalism, state socialism, and the "third world," i.e., the backward countries whose economy is, in non-Marxian terminology, still at the starting point, or, as Marx put it, at the stage of primitive accumulation.

Monopoly capitalism, born of the concentration of capital (the great capitalist organism produced by this concentration being linked more or less permanently in various ways in different countries, giving rise to different types of states controlled by the still-dominant but threatened middle classes)—monopoly capitalism, too, has displayed unforeseen powers of survival and adaptation. This is not the place to analyze this development. Among its many causes, or reasons that may account for it, we shall mention only the challenge of two mutually opposed social and political "systems" facing each other, the stepped-up pace of technological change, and the Second World War. The upheaval caused by this war ended forever the untroubled complacency of a Malthusian-minded middle class huddled over its investments.

Over such a long period the class structure of capitalist society was bound to undergo many changes. New classes and configurations of classes made their appearance while others disappeared; some class lines became blurred, others more clear cut. The process varied according to the different countries involved, their level of economic growth, their political structure, and the circumstances that affected this structure. The very concept of class and its corollary concepts (class consciousness, class psychology, etc.) were modified, obscured, shifted, and given new kinds of emphasis.

We shall set aside all these questions and, instead,

examine the concept of class as treated by Marx, i.e., within the framework of competitive capitalism. Here, as in respect of other matters, we believe that the concepts elaborated by Marx are still necessary but insufficient to understand the human reality of a century later. This is not the place to verify this assertion with reference to our case; the task must be left to other works and other researches.

Why did we not begin with the theory of classes and of the class struggle, calling attention to the sociological aspects of this theory? An approach to Marxian thought from this angle is perfectly conceivable. Actually it is not possible to treat our theme—Marx's sociology—without making repeated reference to the concept of class, the theory of classes and class conflicts. And yet, according to Marx, any society in which polarization into antagonistic classes becomes essential is, historically speaking, a late society, chronologically the last before socialism, namely, capitalist society. Prior to it, every society, each successive stage of social-economic development, has exhibited splits, oppositions, contrasts, conflicts. Wherever such contradictions fail to manifest themselves, society is stagnating or regressing. Social change, whether a progress or a regression, is always determined by internal differences and contradictions. But, before the stage of capitalism is reached, such contradictions or differences are distinguishing features rather than essential conflicts. Let us again call upon feudal society to furnish an example. What characterized it as a whole was the directness, the immediacy of its social relations—they were relations between persons, and hence transparent. Relationships of this type obtained within the family and in all other forms of dependency: from the family group to the village and the lord's demesne. They obtained between the vassal and the suzerain, the serf and the lord—a system of relationships covering the entire range from the lowliest peasant to Almighty God. Being dependent, the peasants could be oppressed, and surplus labor extorted from them in the form of ground rent; to extort this rent, the lords, in addition to their prestige and ascendancy, needed armed troops, which served them also in rivalries among themselves. The system was oppressive, and yet the serf, bound to the soil, could not be separated from the instruments of his labor—his land, his house. Exploitation and oppression ran up against limits in custom. At least to begin with, the lord was the leader of the peasant community, the upholder of custom, judge and dispenser of justice.

Feudal society is thus characterized by its hierarchical organization, not by a polarization of opposing groups. Marx never made the mistake of confusing groups, castes, or classes in process of formation with already constituted classes, polarized classes. Moreover, all history shows that ideologies elaborated by classes still in process of formation (and even by constituted classes) keep a residue of older elements. Class ideologies mask reality by clinging to representations that are historically out of phase. One may go so far as to say, emphasizing this ideological aspect, that the middle class is defined as the class that denies the existence of classes (by stressing the idea of nationality or "society as a whole"). Finally Marx brought to light an especially important process: "the socializing of society." As means of communication and method of exchange steadily increase in number, partitions and particularisms are broken down. It is precisely within societies in process of "socialization" that antagonistic classes make their appearance. The oppositions and contradictions between the classes come to the surface in and through the socializing process and, according to Marx, the deep conflict that results can and must be resolved only by socialism. However, for this to come about, ideologies must not be allowed to mask the situation, to obstruct the process. For all these reasons we discussed the problem of ideology before taking up the problem of social classes.

The polarization of society into essentially antagonistic classes is always accompanied by a so-called economic phenomenon: the generalizing of the commodity, i.e., an ever increasing number of products become commodities. It is once everything can be bought and sold, as we might say, that society divides into two hostile groups—those who sell, and those who fall into the category of saleable "objects," just like things. This formulation, however, is not so clear or explanatory as it may seem. Let us take a closer look at what actually takes place and go back to our basic analysis.

As we have seen, the commodity is a *form*. To grasp this form in its pure state, in the opening pages of *Capital*, Marx deliberately sets aside the chaotic psychological and sociological content in acts of exchange—the needs they satisfy, the parleys and palavers that attend these acts. He proceeds by way of reduction,[33] and this reduction clears the way for a structural analysis. Let us follow this analysis in the first chapter of *Capital*.

"A commodity is, in the first place, an object outside us, a thing that by its properties satisfies human needs of some sort or another. The nature of such needs, whether, for instance, they spring from the stomach or from fancy, makes no difference. Neither are we concerned to know how the object satisfies these needs, whether directly as means of subsistence, or indirectly as means of production."[34]

And in a footnote Marx adds:

" 'things have no intrinsick virtue' (this is Barbon's special term for value in use) 'which in all places have the same virtue; as the loadstone to attract iron.' (Nicolas Barbon, *A Discourse on coining the new money lighter, in answer to Mr. Locke's considerations*, &c. London, 1696, p.6). The property which the magnet possesses of attracting iron became of use only after by means of that property the polarity of the magnet had been discovered."

Marx puts within "brackets" all kinds of properties of things, among them the fact that they correspond to needs and the needs to which they correspond. "The use values of commodities furnish the material for a special study, that of the commercial knowledge of commodities."[35]

The object splits into quality and quantity, matter and form, use value (corresponding to a need, to usefulness, desirability) and exchange value. Once the qualitative aspect, namely the use value of objects, has been set aside by analytic reduction, there remains in them a property which makes it possible to compare them quantitatively: their property of being products of human labor, the result of an expenditure of labor (they embody the average time of social labor needed to produce them, as Marx has shown).

Thus the commodity presents itself as something twofold.

"At first sight a commodity presented itself to us as a complex of two things—use value and exchange value. Later on, we saw also that labor, too, possesses the same twofold nature; for, so far as it finds expression in value, it does not possess the same characteristics that belong to it as a creator of use values. I was the first to point out and to examine critically this twofold nature of the labor contained in commodities."[36]

Things internally split in this way become related and equivalent to other things. More exactly, the relation between our twofold thing and other things is itself twofold. It is the analysis of this dual form that involves difficulties.

The equation $xA = yB$ expresses the fact that a quantity x of the commodity A is equal in value to a quantity y of the commodity B, for instance, 20 yards of linen is worth one coat. The linen expresses its value in the coat; the former commodity plays an active, the latter a passive part; the coat officiates as *equivalent* of the linen, whose value is the *relative* form of value.

"The relative form and the equivalent form are two intimately connected, mutually dependent, inseparable expressions of value; but at the same time are mutually exclusive antagonistic extremes—i.e., poles of the same expression."[37]

Note the terms of the structural analysis Marx carries out here. The dual or twofold form (relative, equivalent) sets two complementary elements against each

other as "mutually exclusive poles." This formal relationship takes the place of the sensuous, physical reality of
the object, and as a result of this substitution the object
is metamorphosed into a commodity, an abstract thing.

As such an abstract thing, the object or product in
question is convertible into a series of different elementary expressions of its value which may be prolonged to
any length: $xA=yB=zC=\ldots$ This series denotes the
equivalence of the time of social labor embodied in the
various objects. It refers to the specific characters of social labor—simple and complex, qualitative and quantitative, etc. The form with its polar structure entails the
dialectical movement of social labor.

> "On the one hand all labor is, speaking physio-
> logically, an expenditure of human labor power, and
> in its character of identical abstract human labor it
> creates and forms the values of commodities. On the
> other hand, all labor is the expenditure of human labor
> power in a special form and with a definite aim, and in
> this, its character of concrete useful labor, it produces
> use values. Just as commodities must first and foremost be
> be values, so labor must first and foremost be useful in
> order to be regarded as an expenditure of human labor
> power in the abstract sense of the word."[38]

However, in this dual form, social labor with its
contradictory determinations is merely implied.[39] The
formal series of commodities with their real links does
remain indefinitely open. In developing it becomes determinate; the fully developed form—the general value
form—expresses the values of all commodities in terms
of a single commodity, which can be any commodity,

but which in social practice bears a well-defined and well-known name—money, gold, or silver.

Let us now try to imagine how this perfectly coherent form functions. "*Qua* values, all commodities are expressions of one and the same unit, human labor, and interchangeable. Consequently, a commodity can be exchanged for another commodity whenever it has a form that makes it appear as a value."[40] The commodities constitute a continuous circuit (commodity—money—commodity—etc.). This circuit is again linked to other similar circuits, the sum total of which is the worldwide circulation of commodities, which goes on endlessly. Each time a commodity disappears, is destroyed by being consumed, another—an equivalent to it—moves into the vacant place. The result is a general equilibrium of exchanges, endangered only when one or several places remain vacant, when links are missing in the chain. In itself the result is harmonious—at least this is the view of economic liberalism, which accepts, puts forward, promotes the circulation of commodities, assuming the automatic self-sufficiency of the market system. For better or worse, however, the view that free trade is self-regulating and results in a harmonious balance of exchanges is untenable. It would be true if the human vehicles of exchange, for instance, were exclusively craftsmen or if all were producing and consuming at the same rate, with tradesmen performing a purely middleman function. Actually, there is one commodity that breaks the circuit and destroys the harmony. This commodity is labor. To make labor a commodity just like the others, taking its place in the endless round of commodity circulation without interrupting it, all that would be needed is for the laborer to sell himself body and soul to anyone who may wish to buy him. This is the situation of the slave or even of the "followers" of a feudal lord. However, in this case, the value of the laborer and his exact place in the endless chain of commodities remain unspecified in the sense that though he does indeed belong body and soul to another, he does not himself buy anything. In order for them to be themselves buyers, i.e., in order to bring about a generalized extension of the commodity, it is necessary that laborers should not be sold. What has the laborer to sell as a commodity? Not himself, not his person, only his labor time, his labor power. Then he remains free and can become part of the continuous circulation of commodities. More exactly, he becomes a part of this continuous circulation as seller and buyer on the one hand, and, on the other hand, as an element in the contractual relationships linking the owners and exchangers of commodities (which add their juridical form to the formal sum of exchange values). Those who have nothing but their "labor" to dispose of thus become links in this two-way endless circuit in two capacities—as producers and buyers on the one hand, and as sellers and contracting parties on the other.

In short, commodities do not assert themselves *qua* things but rather *qua* a kind of logic. It is the form that confers upon them its total character (or, if you will, "totalizes" their capacity to permeate and swallow up everything). It is only by virtue of their form that commodities function as things, as economic fetishes—commodities, gold and silver, capital—and influence human beings.

"The products of labor become commodities, social
things whose qualities are at the same time perceptible
and imperceptible by the senses. . . . But . . . the existence
of the things *qua* commodities and the value relation
of the products of labor which stamps them as commodities, have absolutely no connection with their physical properties and with the material relations arising
therefrom. . . . A definite social relation between men . . .
assumes, in their eyes, the fantastic form of a relation
between things. In order, therefore, to find an analogy,
we must have recourse to the mist-enveloped regions of
the religious world. In that world the productions of the
human brain appear as independent beings endowed
with life, and entering into relation both with one another and with the human race. So it is in the world of
commodities with the products of man's hands. This I
call the Fetishism which attaches itself to the products
of labor, as soon as they are produced as commodities,
and which is therefore inseparable from the production
of commodities."[41]

The thesis of reification[42] misinterprets the essential meaning of the socio-economic theory expounded in
Capital. The fetishes that take on a life of their own,
become autonomous, and impose their laws on interhuman relationships, can function only as *abstract* things
by reducing human beings to the status of abstract
things, by relegating them to the world of forms, reducing them to these forms, to their structures and functions. There is a logic immanent in commodities *qua*
forms, a logic which tends to constitute a world of its
own, the world of commodities. Because this world is
formal, it is related to the formal aspects of language and
rational action, to the logos and logic in the strict sense.

It can be "conveyed" without distorting current language, and it gives rise to a particular type of rationality—the calculating, quantifying type. But is it not possible that as language functions, it leaves its mark on other forms, including the commodity form? The world of commodities makes its way into praxis, penetrating it if not taking it over entirely. Human beings do not become things. This takes place only under slavery (which precedes and remains outside the gradual formation and expansion of the world of commodities) and in prostitution (which has played an important part in the rise of the market economy but is not a distinctive feature of it). What is more likely is that human beings would be turned into animated abstractions, living, breathing, suffering fictions, did they not put up dramatic resistance to this process.

The logic of commodities, however, for all its encroachments upon praxis and its complex interactions with other forms of society and consciousness, does not succeed in forming a permanent, closed system. With its complex determinations, human labor is not entirely taken over by this form, does not become an inherent element of its content. Once set in motion, the endless circuit of exchanges cannot be closed. It gives rise to a movement that sweeps it along, a historical, dialectical movement. Paradoxically, the commodity form can become all-embracing only by giving rise to something else that transcends it. The movement overflows the form with the emergence of men deprived of everything save their labor power—laborers, workers. The commodity they throw on the market is very different from other commodities. It has one uniquely distinctive property: although it can be exchanged, although its value is determined in the market circulation of the commodities by the quantity of social labor needed to produce and reproduce it, yet it creates a value greater than its own in the process of being consumed, in being used. If labor did not have this property of producing surplus value there would be no reason for employing it to operate tools and machinery, results of antecedent labor. This is why labor can no longer be reduced to a set of determinations inherent in the content of the commodity form. It overflows the form, and comes to dominate it. The system of commodity circulation is reorganized once the stage has been reached at which surplus value is produced and capital is accumulated. The commodity form and the contractual form correspond to particular levels of reality in historical societies and specific types of praxis. Such societies and such types of praxis inevitably become polarized: on the one hand, we have those who make use of and manipulate the forms (commodity, money and capital, contracts), on the other, those who possess the active and productive content but only that: namely, labor power. In political economy, the proletarian is defined as the wage laborer who produces capital and makes it bear fruit.[43]

The emergence of classes and the permanent conflict between them are thus construed theoretically starting from forms, functions, and structures, the concepts of which make it possible to give an intelligible meaning to history. The analysis proceeds simultaneously on three planes—that of pure form (logic), that of the relationship between form and content (dialectical logic), and that of social labor with its internal contradictions (dialectical movement, which includes the preceding determinations). As we have anticipated, a sociological reality—a type of praxis—has, so to speak, been born before our eyes, generated by the dialectical relation between form and content, in the historical movement conceived theoretically. We have merely summed up the first hundred pages of *Capital*, discarding superficial interpretations.[44]

The conflict between the bourgeoisie (which controls the means of production comprising the results of past labor—constant capital, machines, raw materials—and the available money, the variable capital which supplies the funds for wages) and the proletariat thus has a foundation in reality. It has become the custom to add the term "objective" to the term "foundation." Why this redundancy? A foundation is objective or it is not a foundation. For that matter, the foundation in our case is subjective, too: it exists in consciousness, i.e., in relations that tend to become conscious. The objective and the subjective factor are inseparable, and the conflicts between the two are an aspect of their underlying unity. At once objective and subjective, the class conflict is perpetual, though sometimes only latent or hidden and sometimes overt and explosive. It never stops, though it sometimes appears to have done so.

Earlier we have assigned to Marxist sociology, claiming this to be Marx's own thought, the task of studying interactions between forms and contents, structures and tendencies, functions and genetic processes. At this point we can clarify our point of view. Marxist sociology can and should take as its object the efforts made by the working class to turn to its advantage the form and laws of exchange value so as to alter the form by making use of and controlling its laws, to prevent the real wages from dropping below the market value of labor power, to achieve a wage above this value, and to increase this value itself (i.e., the needs that must be satisfied in order to reproduce the labor power). Sociology can and should extend its domain to include the efforts of the working class to transcend the laws of value and of the market— the world of commodities—through revolutionary praxis.

This effort of the working class, which can justly be designated as the "class struggle," is continuously going on though not always at the same intensity.

> "The advance of capitalist production develops a working class, which by education, tradition, habit looks upon the conditions of production as self-evident laws of nature. . . . The dull compulsion of economic relations completes the subjection of the laborer to the capitalist. Direct force, outside economic conditions, is of course still used but only exceptionally. In the ordinary run of things, the laborer can be left to the natural laws of production."[45]

The laws in question are none other than those governing exchange value, commodities. When the working class remains passive, they do operate with the force of natural laws. The proletariat has to intervene directly to interrupt the "ordinary run" of abstract things which impose their law. As a rule, the "authorities," the state, step in to restore the ordinary run of things, the smooth working of the law, the ruling classes' power of decision.

The frequently used term "tension" gives only a superficial and distorted image of this reality. What matters is the degree of tension, how dynamically charged it is. By itself the term mistakes effect for cause, and masks the realities underlying the observable phenomena. When this is used instead of such a term as "contradic-

'conflict," or "antagonism," the point of view is ·ely reformist. Such reformism ignores periods of ᴧᴄute struggle, turns its back on the aspiration to transform existing social relations.

It may be useful to recall here that classes and class struggles can be studied at several levels:

[A.]

THE LEVEL OF PRODUCTIVE FORCES AND PRODUCTION RELATIONS

The working class is a productive force. This essential feature is discovered in the production unit, the enterprise. To hold the working class down to this level is to mutilate its reality and its potentialities. The working class is, among other things, a social and political force, to the scale of society as a whole. But first of all it has a production function, which results from the division of labor. As for the bourgeoisie, it endures only by continually unsettling the conditions of production. The moment it stops doing so, the society it dominates is threatened by stagnation, disintegration, parasitism.

"What characterizes the bourgeois epoch is the continual transformation of production, the continual unsettling of all social conditions, insecurity and agitation . . . " says the *Communist Manifesto*. Thus the bourgeoisie swings wildly between a Malthusianism that aims at preserving the *status quo* just as it is, and the furthering of technological innovation. Malthusianism is its ideology in periods of depression, of retreat, when it is on the defensive. Technological snobbery becomes its ideology in periods of expansion, animation, prosperity.

Both ideologies reflect the current level of the productive forces.

The organization of labor is inseparable from tools, machinery, equipment, techniques. If it is necessary to distinguish between a technical and a social division of labor, this would be in order to understand how the one generates the other under given conditions, what distinguishes and what unites them in any well-functioning organization of labor. It entails study of the over-all forms of the division of labor (in each country of the world market and within the given national groups, between agriculture and industry, etc.), without forgetting the special, even singular forms peculiar to a particular workshop. Class distinctions in modern (capitalist) society no longer rest upon craft distinctions; on the contrary, as Marx shows in *Capital*, the division of labor within a single class can give rise to very different modes of labor. The social division of labor modifies the technical division not only because managerial functions are reserved to certain groups (which are actually or virtually part of the bourgeoisie), but also because production as a whole is oriented in accordance with needs it creates or furthers (although not without resistances, contradictions, and conflicts).

Study of production relations in the light of the division of labor discloses a complex, changing class structure in every class society. An essentially identical economic base may, under the influence of various empirical factors, present considerable gradations and variations (Marx), especially in the semi-proletarian strata. In agriculture—which retains some features distinguishing it from industrial production until it, too, attains the level of a big industry—analysis discerns various classes, subclasses, and social strata: tenant farmers, farmers, agricultural laborers, small, medium, and big landowners (linked or not linked with the industrial bourgeoisie). These socio-economic constellations form different groups according to the features of production in the agricultural sector—quantitative or qualitative, specialized or not specialized. Thus, even at the level of productive forces, structure and particular combinations of circumstances interact continually. But the resulting diversity and mobility do not in any way prevent the process of polarization into classes, which remains the pivot of analysis.

> "The owners of mere labor power, the owners of capital, and the landowners, whose respective sources of income are wages, profit, and ground rent, in other words, wage laborers, capitalists, and landowners, form the three great classes of modern society resting upon the capitalist mode of production."[46]

The importance of landowners is steadily decreasing; this class tends to be absorbed into the bourgeoisie of which it is today no more than one stratum, a fraction, a special group, at least in the most highly developed countries.

Analytical study of classes beginning with the technical and social division of labor must be carried forward down to such important though rather elusive differences, for instance, as that between productive and unproductive labor. In discussing Adam Smith, Marx devoted a number of passages to this distinction, most of them little known. Smith applied a narrow, strictly economic criterion to social labor and deliberately confined himself to considering materially productive labor. As for other activities and functions, he tended to assign them to a vague category of "services," falling somewhere outside social labor. According to Marx,[47] the question is far more delicate and complex. Every society, whatever its structure (or mode of production), distributes its productive forces (including its labor power and over-all productivity) in a specific way. It satisfies in a specific way the individual and social needs of its members, needs which it influences, at once creating and setting limits to them (so long as abundance and equality in abundance have not been achieved). Socially the labors of the teacher, the physician, the actor, dispensers of information (newspapermen), and entertainers are as indispensable as those of masons and metal workers. And yet they are not productive of tangible, consumable, material goods. They are necessary for production and yet unproductive. On the other hand, the capitalist mode of production and bourgeois society do not directly pursue the saisfaction of needs, above all, not of social needs. They satisfy needs only indirectly, through the mediation of the market, and only to the extent that the goods to be consumed pass through the commodity stage. More than that: the goal of capitalist production is not production of commodities as such, but profits. In this society labor is productive only to the extent it creates profits for capital and the capitalists. It follows that in this society dominated by the bourgeoisie the labor performed by the artist, the writer, the architect *qua* artist is not (by contrast with the Middle Ages and the Renaissance) regarded as social labor. What determines the value of works of art is a matter of psychological chance, the money at the disposal of those who happen to feel a special need for distraction, amusement, escape.

For all that, a theater, for instance, remains an enterprise in which capital is invested and which is expected to yield profits; the spectators are offered a sort of "goods" which they consume and pay for with income derived from over-all production and surplus value. Another paradox: the production of armaments is classified as productive labor.

The distinction between productive and unproductive labor—a distinction that does not lead to any formal separation—does not coincide with the division between physical or manual labor and intellectual labor.

"In order to labor productively, it is no longer necessary for you to do manual work yourself; enough, if you are an organ of the collective laborer and perform one of its subordinate functions."[48] In other words, it is indeed the division of labor we must look to, both in its technical aspect (relatively independent of the mode of production) and in its social aspect (linked to the mode of production, the over-all features of a given society, its class structure, the activity of the ruling class, and its ideologies). In capitalist society, the "collective laborer" is the aggregate of the production units, the capitalist enterprises, organized for the purpose of producing material goods and, above all, profits.

It follows that, in Marx's view, the nature of the "collective laborer" changes with the over-all character of the given society, with its mode of production. The analysis of various types of labor and of the division of labor in a capitalist society must be modified when we deal with a socialist society. This is especially true in respect of the differences between productive and unproductive labor, socially necessary and socially unnecessary labor.

Technicians such as engineers are productive workers. Agriculture, fishing, the mining industry, the processing industries, the construction and maintenance industry, are all productive activities, also the commercial activities dealing with the preserving, warehousing, and shipping of consumer goods. Other commercial activities, such as advertising, are unproductive. The same goes for material and cultural "services," such as education and scientific research, as well as for the apparatus of government, banking, the armed forces, the police, the bureaucracy, etc.

Without transition and without laying down any criterion for the distinction we have passed from productive to unproductive labor, and from the socially necessary to unnecessary labor, even to leisured unemployment and social parasitism (unless we assume that every activity or "function" is justified by virtue of the mere fact that it exists).

In other words, the distinction Marx made is hard to apply, and yet it is indispensable. It drives analysis into a corner, so to speak, and confronts it with difficult sociological problems—a study both critical and concrete of "functions," "services," of the social mobility that shifts individuals from one category to another, etc.

Marx explicitly rejected sociological "functionalism." In his view it is just another ideology, according to which the various functions in bourgeois society presuppose one another and resolve the internal contradictions of the society, no distinction being made between the technical and the social division of labor, each used to justify the other. This ideology asserts in effect that functions and services are "at the service of" capitalism. This is at once self-evident and absurd, and makes it impossible to elaborate a theory of civilization.[49]

To this lengthy and difficult discussion which turns up again and again we owe one of Marx's most brilliant passages. It deserves to be quoted for its wit and liveliness alone, which scarcely detract from its sociological value, rather the contrary:

> "A philosopher produces ideas, a poet poems, a clergyman sermons, a professor compendia and so on. A criminal produces crimes. If we look a little closer at the connection between this latter branch of production and society as a whole, we shall rid ourselves of many prejudices. The criminal produces not only crimes but also criminal law, and with this also the professor who gives lectures on criminal law and in addition to this the inevitable compendium in which this same professor throws his lectures onto the general market as 'commodities.' This brings with it augmentation of national wealth, quite apart from the personal enjoyment which . . . the manuscript of the compendium brings to its originator himself.
>
> "The criminal moreover produces the whole of the police and of criminal justice, constables, judges, hangmen, juries, etc.; and all these different lines of business, which form equally many categories of the social division of labor, develop different capacities of the human spirit, create new needs and new ways of satisfying them. Torture alone has given rise to the most ingenious mechanical inventions, and employed many honorable craftsmen in the production of its instruments.
>
> "The criminal produces an impression, partly moral and partly tragic, as the case may be, and in this way renders a 'service' by arousing the moral and aesthetic feelings of the public. He produces not only compendia on Criminal Law, not only penal codes along with the legislators in this field, but also art, belles-lettres, novels,

and even tragedies. . . . The criminal breaks the monotony and everyday security of bourgeois life. In this way he keeps it from stagnation, and gives rise to that uneasy tension and agility without which even the spur of competition would get blunted. Thus he gives a stimulus to the productive forces. . . ."[49a]

It would be easy to show that this astonishing fragment contains a "Marxian" commentary on Balzac and his negative hero par excellence, Vautrin. It also shows with what breadth, what a total lack of pedantry, Marx could analyze bourgeois society, its productive forces and its class relations. More particularly, what we must study is the division of labor taken as a whole, without getting entangled in classifications according to sectors, functions, and levels viewed statically (rather than dialectically).

We have repeatedly stressed the importance of forms, of the scientific interest of interactions between forms and contents. Why? Because dogmatists who claim to speak in the name of Marx have long thought themselves obliged to stress contents to the point of ignoring forms. This attitude seemed bound up with philosophical materialism, and actually was to the extent that this materialism doubled as a philosophico-political system. The term "form" was given only a superficial, extraneous meaning. Form in the full sense of the term, the term it has in the expression "formal logic," was misunderstood and neglected. The commodity form was no longer understood as such, no more than political, juridical, aesthetic, or philosophical form. It was forgotten that a content is a content only by taking on form, and that the dialectical interplay between form and content is a matter of the most essential importance.

Can it be said that the *social* division of labor supplies a form, which is defined by the mode of production, to the *technical* division of labor? Certainly. Productive forces are the content of production relations, the latter tending to hold the productive forces within their nets, while the productive forces at the same time try to loosen their hold or break free. Production relations (including the market, wage labor, the power of money and capital) are not something apart from productive forces, but constitute a dialectical unity, marked by conflicts. Though the sociological factor cannot be separated from the strictly economic factor, the two are not identical. This assertion will not be true once the social and the technical division of labor have come to coincide. Some technocrats assume that this is already the case. They believe that with the growing predominance of technology, socio-economic reality, whether we call it capitalist or socialist, is moving closer to a state of balance which does away with the conflicts Marx described and analyzed. We cannot go into this matter here; we shall merely observe that on this score technocratic utopianism is especially vulnerable to criticism. It is possible to show that decisions are not invariably or exclusively determined by technological reasons, that the strategic variables still depend on the over-all character of the society and the mode of production, and that technology has not supplanted social relationships nor solved their inherent conflicts. In other words, a sociology bound up with Marx's thought and the Marxian outlook has not yet, we believe, lost its validity. More than that: it must be restored in all its analytic vigor, rather than be replaced with empiricism pure and simple or with an ideology (such as technocracy).

[B.]

THE LEVEL OF PROPERTY AND JURIDICAL RELATIONS

No society is a mere aggregate of functions. Over and above the social and economic functions and the form they take as a whole, another set of forms is required to keep them in existence and regularize them—rules, norms, "values," juridical principles. This is true of every society, but especially of capitalist society. The rule of commodities has its counterpart in the rule of contracts. The multiple contractual bonds between the members of this society (including "the labor contract") are in contrast with the multiple conflicts that characterize it. More than any other, such a society needs a legal code (or codes plus subsidiary codes). The rise of the bourgeoisie and the formation of capitalism are thus reflected in the elaboration and promulgation of the Napoleonic *Code Civil.* This Code formalizes, institutionalizes the property relations inherent in existing production relations. Inspired by Roman law, the Code analyzes and gives coherent, quasi-logical form to aspects of the contract. Bourgeois society is asserted and confirmed in it only in a disguised fashion, implicit in the form. The world of commodities appears in it only in its counterpart—the endless chain of interlocking contractual relations.

Marx and Engels put great emphasis on the importance of Roman law. It has persisted—not without modifications and adjustments—through a number of modes of production, a number of societies (slavery, feudalism, capitalism, and even socialism), thus showing that it cannot be classified as a mere "superstructure" or institution. As a form of human relations it has a foundation deeper and more lasting than production relations. It regulates interindividual and intergroup relations so long as society is dominated by commodity exchange, and so long as the products of social labor are not sufficiently abundant to be distributed evenly. Legal justice is the corollary of injustice. *Summmum ius, summa iniuria.* Be that as it may, juridical form is not isolated from the other basic forms, which have been imposed upon human contents, products, works, activities—formal logic, the commodity form, the forms of language and discourse.

Thus the Code has immense importance. A narrow functionalism does not discriminate between functions as they appear at the socio-economic level and the same functions as they are formulated and standardized in the Code. Without it bourgeois society outside the capitalist production units would be a chaos of individual efforts and rival interests. The Code introduces order into this chaos of atoms and monads by giving coherent form to its immanent principles, namely, those governing private property.

Thus the Code makes it possible to decipher the hidden sense of bourgeois society. It provides us with a key, discloses its specific features and basic alienations (for instance, the split between the private and the public sectors, between the man and the citizen, between the reality of selfishness and the fiction of community).

Although the Code aims at a formal coherence similar to that of logic, it is characterized by a degree of elasticity, a certain capacity for adaptation. The legal codes promulgated in different countries and by different nations are not identical, though they are based on common principles. Moreover subsidiary codes make their appearance. These act upon the basic Code, sooner or later merge with it or modify it. In this way, alongside the Napoleonic Code, and even at its expense, the rights of various existing social categories were drawn up—the rights of workers, women, children, the old, the sick.

The subsidiary codes merely reform the basic Code; a revolution would abrogate it though some of its elements would be preserved in an altered form. A socialist society is still characterized by contracts and legal rights. According to Marx, it cannot transcend "the narrow horizon of bourgeois law," the odd mixture of formal equalities and actual inequalities this law regulates. Only a communist society, a society of plenty governed by the maxim "To each according to his needs, from each according to his capacities," will be able to dispense with a formal body of laws, norms, formal maxims, and gradually, in unforeseen ways, go back to the rule of custom. Until this historical moment has been reached, juridical sociology, the formalized sociological study of institutions, will remain an especially important aspect of the study of class relations, i.e., of a properly Marxian sociology.

Codified juridical relations characterize the structure of a society that admits inequalities. They express the production relations as a formal system, and in this sense we may speak of a "capitalist" or a "socialist" system, but we must keep in mind that the inherent contradictions are not thereby eliminated but are merely attenuated, subjected to a norm. Incomplete, unsatisfactory solutions are put forward, but these do not resolve the conflicts. The systematizing and structure imposed go no deeper than a certain level below which the "base" preserves a reality of its own. The latter shows itself from time to time in unanticipated difficulties, problems, technological and economic changeabouts, including depressions and financial crises. Meanwhile, over the juridical structure superstructures arise to re-interpret, to take over, and to impose new forms on such contents as cannot be contained by the structure proper. It is crude and naive to view such "systems" or "structures" as literally representing "functions." In real societies, i.e., at the level of praxis, such terms are neither so all-inclusive nor comprehensive as they appear: there are glaring gaps, distortions, areas of social reality they fail to "cover." The powers-that-be keep fiddling empirically with all these elements, plugging up old gaps while new forms are emerging. To ignore the concept of totality is just as unsatisfactory as to take it literally, logically instead of dialectically.

[c.]

THE LEVEL OF POLITICAL SUPERSTRUCTURES

We merely mention this point here; it will be treated in the next chapter on Marxian political sociology, i.e., the theory of the state.

[D.]

THE IDEOLOGICAL LEVEL

Here, following Marx, we shall develop one specific example: the ideology of individualism. The individual capitalist sees himself as the personal owner of his capital, whether this consists of money, control over means of production, constant capital (machines, raw materials) or variable capital (funds for paying wages and salaries). He sees his enterprise as the result of his own efforts, his own flair for business. Now, if this were really the case, society could not function for a moment. It would break up into separate pieces, or rather would never emerge from chaos in the first place, would remain a formless aggregate of atoms, of monads. Marxian analysis shows how and why general laws and even overall self-regulatory mechanisms result from the interactions between separate efforts of private individuals: the formation of an average rate of profit, the more or less brutal elimination of enterprises unable to compete, progressive capital accumulation (interrupted by depressions and slumps which purge the system of its surpluses).

What, then, does individualism signify? A mixture of reality and illusion. It is hard for capitalists to grasp the actual results of what they do. Even calling upon the resources of knowledge and power, they find it hard to explore the market, and even harder to master it. Individualism is illusory. It is a concomitant to individual failure no less than to the dubious success of a few in accumulating money and capital. And yet individualism is not pointless in bourgeois society. It stimulates energies. It plugs up existing gaps in reality, life, culture. It gives confidence. It conceals intolerable aspects of reality and exalts aspects acceptable to the bourgeois. It enables the bourgeois to stand on their "dignity," to believe themselves human amid the inhumanity they profit from and sustain. It has a great many ethical and aesthetic advantages. Moreover, it outlines a general form of individual fulfillment, a form which in bourgeois society remains purely potential and without content. Only another kind of society can realize the individuality anticipated, conceived of, dreamed of by the bourgeois epoch. Finally, and this is not the least important feature, individualism supplies a world view capable of surviving the conditions that created it. Individualism does not disappear with the competitive capitalism that brought it into the world. Although "organizational" capitalism with its giant production and management units, and its bureaucracy, ought to relegate individualism among the obsolete ideologies, this world view still serves as a stimulus, as a weapon against other, more adequate views, alternatively a veil over reality and its justification.

The sociology of ideological forms tries to discover their class meaning in a dialectical manner, i.e., at manifold levels both in the past and the present, studying the conditions for their emergence, their points of impact, their rebirths and renewals, their truly representative and their illusion-creating functions alike, the shifts among them, cynical utilizations of them, etc. The critique of ideologies deepens the distinction between appearance and reality. We learned long since that there is no such thing as social "reality" pure and simple. There is no reality that does not produce appearances, no praxis (save perhaps the creative praxis of great revolutionary periods) that does not generate illusions. In every society the appearances are part of reality, and the illusions are part of the praxis. In some cases the unreal is real, and vice versa. Thus, the dialectical method enables us to assert the concept of the real and to include the formal in it.

The sociological study of ideologies climaxes that of classes and class relationships. In the course of the latter the concept of ideology turns up again and again. Every ideology systematizes (formalizes) an aggregate of illusions, mutilated and distorted representations which nonetheless retain sufficient reference to "reality" (praxis) to appear true, to find a place in this reality, to be experienced. If they did not, there would be no such thing as ideology, only the crudest deceit. The analysis of ideologies finds its proper place in the study of forms that impose a certain order—a relative, precarious order, often put in question—on the constitutive elements of class society.

To the dialectical method of analysis and exposition, such as is exemplified in Marx's *Capital,* form at a certain level becomes content at a higher level. In this way, the juridically formalized relationships serve as elements, as contents for the reflection that constructs ideologies.

The ideological form completes this hierarchization. At this level analysis can thematize the elements available to it. It can devote itself to criticism of a given ideology—study the aggregate of ideologies and "values" that constitute a "culture"—and it can also devote itself to the theory of what is called "civilization," which has barbarism as its obverse, a barbarism that in some respects is on the increase in the so-called "modern" world.

In the foregoing we have tried not to separate the static from the dynamic, the structural from the conjunctural elements, the analytic elements from the whole, the genetic from the actual, the "diachronic" from the "synchronic." None of these terms and antitheses is absolutely adequate. All of them contain ideological elements mixed up with the conceptual thinking. However, out of all of them and the unity of the opposing aspects a conception of history emerges as a process that gives rise to relative stabilities, then transcends them, and dissolves them and breaks them up. This is Marx's conception, though he never completely formulated it. By its nature the dialectical method must unite the different aspects, the successive "moments" of Becoming. The unity excludes neither the theoretical oppositions nor the real-life struggles. On the contrary, it includes them.

Needless to say, we have not exhausted the sociological aspects of the Marxian theory of classes. Before concluding this chapter, let us underline once more a few fundamental assertions. First point: there are no classes without class struggles, without political struggles. A class exists only virtually (it exists "in itself," not "for itself") so long as it has not made its entrance on the political stage, at a higher level of praxis, with a revolutionary praxis. Second point: the classes polarized in conflict or struggle at the same time constitute a unity. This unity is given an over-all designation ("society"), a special designation ("a nation") or a more detailed designation (the division of labor that obtains in the actual units of production). The conflicts allow us to lay stress on the unity; conversely, once we have laid stress on unity, we should elucidate the antitheses underlying it.

The constellation of classes and fractions of classes, i.e., the structure of society, changes with historical circumstances. In his *Revolution and Counter-Revolution in Germany*, Marx enumerates eight classes: the feudal groups, the bourgeoisie, the petty bourgeoisie, the big and medium farmers, the small peasants, the serfs, the agricultural workers, the industrial workers. In his *Class Struggles in France*, however, he considers seven classes: the financial bourgeoisie, the industrial bourgeoisie, the mercantile bourgeoisie, the petty bourgeoisie, the peasants, the proletariat, the lumpenproletariat. In other words, in about the same period (1848) the social structures of two unequally developed societies, yet both on the road to capitalism, exhibited notable differences. Structural analysis must leave scope for the march of events, constantly changing circumstances.

A revolution is the consequence of a structure, but the revolutionary event depends on a conjunction of circumstances.

The classes Marx described and analyzed as essential to competitive capitalism, namely, landowners, industrial capitalists, and workers, draw their incomes from three sources—ground rent, profits, wages. However, not every landowner's income is produced by his farmers, tenant farmers, and agricultural laborers any more than every capitalist's is produced by his own workers. The aggregate of surplus value produced falls within a larger category—the national income as a whole. Marx intended to conclude his major work, *Capital*, with a theory of income and the way it is distributed. Production and property relationships as they actually obtain in society are technical devices comparable to pumps—for sucking in as great a part as possible of the over-all surplus product. The process of distribution is determined by the nature of society as a whole. The notion that "the capitalist exploits his workers" is crude and naive. It is the bourgeoisie as a class that exploits the proletariat as a class (and the other classes, fractions of classes, and groups) by getting into its hand the greatest possible share of the national income; it does this in various ways —economically, socially, politically, administratively, fiscally, and even culturally (through its organization of leisure activities and artistic production). The income is distributed through the intermediary of the social whole, the state—such is the central idea of the last section of *Capital*. The various parts of the ruling class act as pressure groups, making use of legislation, for example. The Marxian analysis of classes has to be situated within the over-all framework if it is to be referable to sociology to the same extent economics is.

Unfortunately *Capital* is an unfinished work: the exposition which was to have concluded the structural and historical analysis remains incomplete. If the founder of Marxian thought had been able to complete his task, had he written the treatise on dialectical methodology he projected in the second half of his life, and thereby given the finishing touches to his socio-economic theory of capitalist society, many subsequent misunderstandings would have been avoided.

5
Political Sociology: Theory of the State

The theory of the state is the core or, if you will, the culmination of Marxian thought. Very naturally, from the outset it has led to particularly passionate controversies. No other aspect of Marxian thought has been so greatly blurred, distorted, and befogged as this.

Marx began to formulate his ideas about the state in his earliest critical essays on the Hegelian philosophy of right and the state. Against Hegel, Marx maintains that the essence of man is not political but social. Man is not a political animal. The social forces that blindly seek a way out of their conflicts become subject to the political power, the state. Social relations, including contradictions that give rise to class struggles, account for the state, not the other way round, as it seemed to Hegel. This fundamental criticism is aimed by Marx at every political form in turn. The very existence of the state presupposes that men make their history without knowing how or why, implies a certain lack of consciousness, of rationality, of organization in society. Moreover, the modern state is founded upon the fact that human reality is split into public life and private life, into citizens and individuals. This split accounts for the political alienation and must be abolished.

According to Marx, then, the state does not express some transcendent rationality, superior to social life, nor is it inherent in society, an expression of its immanent rationality. State and the interests of the state are rooted in an irrational, immature social reality. The state is but a fragment of society that sets itself above society, adding to the functions which are socially indispensable at a given epoch, supererogatory functions made possible by the exercise of power. Those in power seize hold of the rationality inherent in the existing praxis; taking advantage of its incomplete character, they divert it to their own purposes and turn it, if need be, against society as a whole. Setting itself above society, the state has interests of its own and its own social support, namely, its own employees, its bureaucracy. It holds multiple powers—organization, ideology, constraint, political decision. But it cannot be entirely separated from the actual society on which it is based—the classes and their struggles. It has a distinct reality, but this reality is not autonomous, though it tends to autonomy; its reality depends on the existing social relationships. Consequently, although the state apparatus tends to set itself above classes, it cannot remain aloof from them and their struggles. It serves the ruling class or classes, and at the same time acts as arbiter of their rivalries whenever they threaten the

society's existence. Thus it is at once political battle-
ground and the victor's spoils.

Though Marx did not make fully explicit his ideas
on this score, in his view the separation of powers characteristic of the modern state corresponds merely to a
specific stage of the division of labor and social functions generally. More exactly, it is an aspect of the
division of labor, which is superimposed over the technological division, and which modifies and transforms the
latter. Human unity, dissociated at the individual, social,
economic, and political levels, will be restored only
when society as a whole, transformed by revolutionary
action, has absorbed the state, organized economic life,
and enabled the individual to reconstruct himself on new
foundations, without legal systems or other external con-
straints. Economy, society, politics are thus aspects,
levels, elements or "moments" of reality. These "moments" are distinct, though they are not separate entities. None of these levels can lay claim to eternal truth.
The social level, however, can lay claim to a historically
founded priority. In respect of the state, the revolutionary movement which guides the working class will have
three inseparable objectives: development of democracy,
dictatorship of the proletariat, withering away of the
state. The dictatorship of the proletariat means concrete
democracy, i.e., the coercive power of a majority over a
minority. The working class must destroy the machinery
of the existing state, but its own state is to last only for a
transitional period during which the state functions of
organization and management are taken over by new
social forces. Existing state authorities replace rational
organization with coercion, negate human freedom by
their very nature. The justification and legitimacy of such

coercion will disappear, and the state will begin to wither away when a truly rational organization of production becomes possible.

In short, Marxian thought is fundamentally anti-state. The theory of state socialism, according to which the state is the manager of economic life and the higher principle of society, was advanced by a man against whom Marx fought bitterly: Ferdinand Lassalle. It is well known that Lassalle negotiated with Bismarck, and that they were in agreement concerning their long-range objectives, namely, to get the state recognized by the working class, to integrate the latter in the state, and to limit the working class's social and political activity. In a sense we may say that Bismarck—along with Lenin but at the opposite pole—was the greatest political genius of recent modern times. Authoritarian but efficient regimes, which seek to carry out what Marx and Engels called "revolution from above," are closer to Bismarckism than to French Bonapartism.

Given the importance of the question, let us take it up from the beginning. Let us re-read the early works of Marx, the so-called "philosophical" works, which actually contain a radical criticism of philosophy and politics—both were intimately linked in the Hegelian system.

In the essay entitled "A Critique of the Hegelian Philosophy of Right" (1843) Marx writes:

"The criticism of German juridical and political philosophy, which has received through Hegel its most consistent, most ample, and most recent shape, is at once the critical analysis of the modern state and of the actuality which is connected therewith."[50]

No question about it, what we have here is the critical analysis of the modern state, not merely of Hegelian philosophy, though the latter represents its most elaborate theorization. Marx began his career with this criticism of political reality.

"In addition [this criticism is a] decisive repudiation of the entire previous mode of the German political and juridical consciousness, whose principal and most universal expression, elevated to the level of a science, is speculative jurisprudence itself.

"While, on the one hand, speculative jurisprudence, this abstract and exuberant thought-process of the modern state, is possible only in Germany, on the other hand, the German conception of the modern state, making abstraction of real men, was only possible because and in so far as the modern state itself makes abstraction of real men or only satisfies the whole of man in an imaginary manner."[51]

The meaning of the last sentence quoted is that political man, the citizen—the political citizen—is no more than a political fiction in which real man, the whole man, only fulfills himself fictitiously. A political form, a state fiction, is added to the ideological, juridical, and other fictions or is superimposed on them. Man will realize his potentialities not at the level of the state, in the state, or in what depends on the state, but by freeing himself from the state. The formulation could not be clearer.

In "On the Jewish Question," dating from about the same time (Marx was twenty-five), we read:

"Only where the political state exists in its completeness can the relation of the Jew, of the religious man generally, to the political state, and therefore the relation of religion to the state, be studied in its special features and in its purity. The criticism of this relationship ceases to be theological criticism when the state ceases to adopt a theological attitude towards religion, when its attitude towards religion becomes purely political. The criticism then becomes criticism of the political state."[52]

And Marx goes on to say: "Political emancipation from religion is not thorough-going and consistent emancipation from religion, because political emancipation is not effectual and consistent human emancipation," i.e., where the Church has been separated from the state we have merely an emancipation, not a complete liberation. In other words, political emancipation and freedom coincide only partially; the former leads in the direction of freedom, yet is only a degree or historical stage in that process. Political emancipation is limited because the state can free itself from a limitation without man being really freed thereby; a state may become free, and yet its citizens remain unfree. This is true of all states that achieve independence, all new states, for instance; the people's belief that once they have achieved national independence they will immediately become free is an illusion. Consequently a state may be emancipated from religion, and yet the great majority of its citizens may still profess religious faith. The relation between the state, more particularly, between the "free" state and religion, is nothing but a relation between the men who constitute the state and the existing religions. Man frees himself from one particular limitation through the intermediary of the state, i.e., politically, but he himself rises above this limitation only in a limited way: when he declares he is an atheist through the intermediary of the state, i.e., when he declares that the state is atheistic, he remains religiously limited. The state interposes itself between man and human freedom; at best, when the state throws off one or another fetter, such as a state religion, this is no more than an intermediate stage in the realization of man's essence.

In an important passage of the same essay Marx criticizes the internal split within the political state between man and the citizen, between the private man and the public man, a split which also introduces division between the individual and society, and between the individual and himself:

> "The individual leads not only in thought, in consciousness, but in reality, a double life, a heavenly and an earthly life, a life in the political community, wherein he counts as a member of the community, and a life in civil society, wherein he is active as a private person, regarding other men as a means, degrading himself as a means and becoming a plaything of alien powers. The political state is related to civil society as spiritualistically as heaven is to earth."[53]

This applies to the political state which has attained its complete development, i.e., the most modern, the most democratic state. The state is essentially of the same nature as religion even when it has set itself apart from religion and fights against it. There is a state religiosity inseparable from the very existence of the state because the state is in the same relation to real life as heaven to earth: it is above real life, it soars or seems to soar above it. It subdues real life in the same way as religion overcomes the limitations of the profane world.

> "Man in his outermost reality, in civil society, is a profane being. Here, where he is a real individual for himself and others, he is an untrue phenomenon. In the state, on the other hand, where the individual is a generic being, he is the imaginary member of an imagined sovereignty; he is robbed of his real individual life and filled with an unreal universality."[54]

Marx criticizes the splitting up of rights into the rights of man and the rights of the citizen. Man and his consciousness are thereby torn between all-embracing political, juridical, and philosophical fictions on the one hand, and narrow, limited realities on the other. The rights of the citizen are abstract, fictitious. All they grant the individual is an imaginary sovereignty within an unreal universality; as for the rights of man, they are in effect the rights of the selfish individual and, in bourgeois society, they come down to the right of ownership of private property.

> "In the moments of heightened consciousness, the political life seeks to suppress its fundamental conditions, civil society and its elements, and to constitute itself as the real and uncontradictory generic life of the individual. It is, however, only enabled to do this by a flagrant violation of its conditions of life, by declaring the revolution to be permanent."[55]

Political life crushes everyday life, economic life, the life of real individuals. It destroys its own conditions when it seems to become more intense, when it sets itself above ordinary everyday life. It negates its own prerequisites "by declaring the revolution to be permanent." The "permanent revolution" ends inevitably in the restoration of religion, private property, and the elements of civil society, just as war ends in peace. Marx obviously was thinking of Jacobinism here, but what is in question is of far wider relevance. The concept of "permanent" or "total" revolution preoccupies, even obsesses Marx. He sometimes acclaims and proclaims it, sometimes distrusts it. The text quoted here is directed against the state, politics as such. History has known periods in which political life was so intense that it destroyed its own conditions of existence, when permanent revolution led to restoration of the *status quo ante* and "depoliticalization."

> "The members of the political state are religious by virtue of the dualism between individual life and the generic life, between the life of civil society and the political life; they are religious to the extent that the individual regards as his true life the political life beyond his real individuality."[56]

Marx's critique is directed against political life itself:

> "Religion is here the spirit of civil society, the expression of the separation and the alienation of man from man. The political democracy is Christian to the extent that it regards every individual as the sovereign, the supreme being, but this really signifies the individual in his uncultivated, unsocial aspect, the individual in his fortuitous existence, the individual just as he is, the individual as he is destroyed, lost, and alienated through the whole organization of our society, as he is given under the dominance of inhuman conditions and elements, in a

word, the individual who is not yet a real generic being. The sovereignty of the individual, as an alien being distinguished from the real individual, which is the chimera, the dream, and the postulate of Christianity, is under democracy sensuous reality, the present, and the secular maximum."[57]

On several occasions Marx developed the thesis according to which democracy is to other forms of the state as Christianity is to other religions. Christianity places man at the summit, but this man is alienated. Similarly, democracy places man at the summit, but this man is alienated, too, not the real, fully developed man. Why? Because democracy is a political state.

Marx's criticism of the "rights of man" takes a similar line. The rights of man, he observes, are distinguished from the rights of the citizen. But what is man as distinguished from the citizen? Nothing other than a member of civil society. Why is the member of civil society called "man" pure and simple, and why are his rights called "the rights of man"? What can account for this?

"The so-called rights of man, as distinguished from the rights of the citizen, are nothing else than the rights of the member of civil society, that is, of the egoistic individual, of man separated from man and the community. . . . The freedom in question is the freedom of the individual as an isolated atom thrown back upon himself. . . . The right of man to freedom is not based upon the connection of man with man, but rather on the separation of man from man. It is the right to this separation, the right of the individual limited to himself."[58]

The practical application of the right of man to freedom, Marx goes on to say, is his right to private property, and hence, the right to enjoy and dispose of his property at will, without regard for others, independently of society. It is the right of self-interest. Individual freedom in this sense is the basis of civil society. As a result, every man finds in other men not the realization but rather the limitation of his freedom. In short, none of the so-called rights of man goes beyond the egoistic individual.

"Political man is only the abstract, artificial individual, the individual as an allegorical, moral person. . . . All emancipation leads back to the human world, to human relationships, to men themselves. Political emancipation is the reduction of man, on the one side, to the egoistic member of civil society, to the egoistic, independent individual, on the other side to the citizen, to the moral person. . . .

"Not until the real, individual man is identical with the citizen, and has become a generic being in his empirical life, in his individual work, in his individual relationships, not until man has recognized and organized his own capacities as social capacities so that the social energies are no longer divided by the political power, not until then will human emancipation be achieved."[59]

Not until individual man has reconquered himself, has put an end to political alienation, has recovered the social energies taken away from him, and has become a social being *qua* individual—not until he has recognized and organized his own energies as social energies (and we shall presently see the exact meaning of these terms), i.e., when the political form and power (the state) no longer exist outside him, above him—not until then is human (as distinguished from political) emancipation achieved. The road leading to freedom is full of obstacles and accidents, especially the political emancipations that are mistaken for true liberations.

Let us turn now to Marx's critical notes on Hegel's philosophy of the state, dating from 1843.[60] "The actual relationship of the family and civil society to the state," he writes, "is conceived of by Hegel as their *inner, imaginary activity*." In actual fact, family and civil society are presupposed by the state, whereas in Hegel's speculation this relationship is inverted. When you assert that the "subject" is the Idea—i.e., a mind or even a supermind, an absolute—the real subjects, such as civil society, families, and any or all actual circumstances become unreal "moments" of the Idea. This is a clear example of Hegel's panlogical mysticism, of how he hypostatizes the absolute Idea. Hegel does not take the object as his point of departure; he deduces the objective world from an Idea that is intrinsically complete in the realm of logic. In this way, concludes Marx, the political categories spring into existence as the most abstract logicometaphysical categories.

"Hegel starts from the state and makes man the subjectivized state; democracy starts from man and makes the state the objectivized man. Just as it is not religion that creates man, but man who creates religion, so the constitution does not create the people, but the people create the constitution. In a sense, democracy is to all political forms what Christianity is to all other religions. . . .

"Democracy is the essence of all state constitutions, it is socialized man as the constitution of a *specific* state; it is to other constitutions as the genus to its species,

only here the genus itself appears as an existent, and
hence as a particular species. . . . In monarchies, for
example, or republics . . . political man has his particular
existence side by side with nonpolitical, private man.
Property, marriage, contracts, civil society . . . here play
the part of contents, and the state that of pure form."[61]

Hegel, then, views the state as a form that organizes
a formless content. Without the state the content would
relapse into chaos. This conception of the state, derived
from Hegel, is still frequently put forward in our own
day.

"In democracy," Marx goes on to say, "the political
state itself . . . is merely a particular content, something
like the particular way of life of its people. . . . The
modern French interpreted this in the sense that in a
true democracy the state is eliminated." Complete and
true democracy is not merely a political regime superior
to others, but implies the disappearance of political
democracy itself, i.e., of the state. On this score Marx
takes up and develops an idea advanced by Saint-Simon.
According to the latter's well-known parable, if any ten
statesmen, ten generals, and ten princes were suddenly
abducted from any country, the country would keep on
functioning exactly as before. But if the ten leading scientists, the ten leading technicians, and the ten leading
industrialists were abducted, society could no longer
function.

At the time, this idea was "in the air" in France,
thanks largely to Saint-Simon's writings. Marx's criticism
of Hegel is not confined to the theory of the state;
his aim is not merely to replace it with his own theory of
the state: his criticism foreshadows also his theory of
the withering away of the state, of its eventual dis-

appearance from history. It is a fundamental criticism, which goes much farther than mere analysis plus a few objections.

Marx devotes several pages of his critical notes to Hegel's "estates," i.e. partial groups such as trades, corporations, the family, etc. Among these Hegel mentions a propertyless "estate" dependent on "concrete" labor. This "estate," Marx observes, is more than just a part of civil society—in the modern state it is the foundation upon which all other "estates" rest.

Concerning the relations between the Estates and the Executive, Hegel wrote:

> "It is important . . . to emphasize this aspect of the matter because of the popular, but most dangerous prejudice which regards the Estates principally from the point of view of their opposition to the Executive, as if that were their essential attitude. If the Estates become an organ of the whole by being taken into the state, they evince themselves solely through their mediating function. In this way their opposition to the Executive is reduced to a show. . . . If they were opposed not merely superficially, but actually and in substance, then the state would be in the throes of destruction."[62]

What Hegel is trying to say, is that the "Estates" —corporations, trades, we might say today, labor unions, in short, the components of civil society—are not really opposed to the government, and that to think otherwise is a dangerous mistake. They must be viewed as organs of the whole, i.e., integrated in the higher category of the state. Thus conciliation comes to the fore, conflict moves to the background. Hegel himself sees that if the contradictions between the components of civil society and the state were real, the state would be undermined and eventually destroyed. Marx carries Hegel's insight a step farther.

Criticism of the state (including the democratic state) is very explicitly and emphatically linked by Marx with criticism of philosophy and goes far beyond mere criticism of the Hegelian system. Both state and political institutions, he notes, are "representative." Now, "representation" (whether we take the term in the philosophical or the political sense) is always abstract in relation to concrete human beings. In science abstract concepts are gradually narrowed down, corrected, verified, and modified to grasp reality more fully and concretely. Political representation, however, is modified only politically, i.e., in the course of real action, actual struggles connected with society's political needs and the pressures of social forces. Here the process has a more dramatic character than in theoretical knowledge. The abstract character of political representation (the people's representatives and their representative institutions) can be palliated through reform, but never overcome. Revolutionary praxis does not aim merely at reforming the representative systems, but at abolishing them and replacing them with the rational management of things and human freedom, and with transparent, direct relationships between men.

Philosophical representations are just as abstract as political representation, and this abstractness is not the only thing they have in common. On the one hand, the concepts of freedom, justice, consciousness, rationality have both political and philosophical connotations, elements borrowed from both reality (praxis) and ideologies. Philosophy can be realized, the true and the good

can enter into praxis only if freedom is more than political representation and justice more than a political ideal,
in other words, only when democracy fulfills its aspirations and goals, going beyond its own political institutions. On the other hand, philosophical representations
have always been bound up with political groups: it is in
this sense that philosophy is ideological. More particularly, the great bureaucracies—those of the Church as
well as those of the state—have given rise to systems. A
bureaucracy needs an ontology. Materialism and its opposite, spiritualism, were the expression of, and served as
the justification for, machineries of state which required
the elaboration of a metaphysics.[63] Thus the theory of
the abolition (i.e., realization) of philosophy is closely
connected with the theory of the abolition of the supreme political abstraction, the withering away of the
state.

According to Marx, there is no such thing as "true
democracy." To him the sense of democracy is that it
discloses the truth of politics. He sees it not as a system
but as a process which comes down essentially to a
struggle for democracy. The latter is never completed
because democracy can always be carried forward or
forced back. The purpose of the struggle is to go beyond
democracy and beyond the democratic state, to build a
society without state power.

Of special interest to political sociology today are
Marx's notes on bureaucracy. Max Weber is frequently
credited with having first drawn attention to the importance of bureaucracy and having initiated its analysis.
And indeed his achievement is the more impressive for
the fact that he did not know Marx's critical notes on

Hegel's philosophy of the state. Marx did anticipate Weber: he was the first to subject bureaucracy to a critical study, taking as his point of departure Hegel's praise of it.

According to Hegel the "Civil servants and the members of the executive constitute the greater part of the middle class, the class in which the consciousness of right and the developed intelligence of the mass of the people is found."[64] He goes on to argue that the state should therefore favor the middle class; it is best served when it has a competent devoted officialdom whose powers—in the case of their misuse—are limited by the rights of the other components of civil society. Thus directly below the cultivated class, the elite of which fill the ministries, we have the rights of the corporations. Above that class are the political institutions and the sovereign. Below it fall the various groups of special interests. Above it is the general interest represented by the state and the government. Thus Hegel starts from the premise that the state is distinct from civil society (i.e., the "Estates," the "corporations," and the crafts or trades —which in his day described the chief divisions of civil society), and assigns to a bureaucracy the role of mediator between the two.

"And that's all there is to it!" Marx observes ironically. Hegel contents himself with an empirical description of bureaucracy. This description of how the modern state functions is in part objective, and in part reflects the favorable opinion bureaucracy has of itself. Hegel does not criticize it in depth, does not go beyond purely formal considerations, never inquiring into the content, whereas here more than elsewhere, form is inseparable from content. The fact is, according to Marx, bureaucracy comes down to a "formalism" applied to a content outside it.[65]

Interrelations among social groups account for their "representations," i.e., the way they see and understand themselves (or rather, misunderstand themselves). These representations are only partly rational, they do not adequately express the knowledge society or even any privileged group within it has of itself. It is only too true that the social division of labor—superimposed on the technological division—provides the bureaucracy with its basis, namely, the separation between particular and general interests, between private life and public life. We are aware of this, and Hegel recognized it in his fashion, but Hegel sanctions this separation, this split, by assuming that social relationships and representations developed on this foundation are just and true. He takes for granted the complete, definitive rationality of this state of affairs, although his own analysis of it proves the opposite. The existence of bureaucracy presupposes the existence of separate social units linked by means extraneous to their internal organization. As a result, the bureaucracy sees the corporations and estates as its material counterpart; the corporations and estates see the bureaucracy as their ideal counterpart. The ideas they have of each other are "ideological," though in the text under discussion Marx does not yet use this term. He uses philosophical terms: "The corporations are the materialism of bureaucracy, and the bureaucracy is the spiritualism of the corporations."[66] Actually, within civil (nonpolitical) society, the state is itself a corporation. The two social forms presuppose each other, overlap, refer to, and justify each other.

In Hegel's philosophy these relationships are presented as rational and harmonious. Actually, this philosophy is ideological, it masks and disguises reality. And
yet the conflicts show through. Where a bureaucracy is
set, the state interest (represented by this bureaucracy)
becomes a distinct entity which encompasses both the
special interests of the corporations and the other social
bodies *and* the so-called general interest, i.e., that of
society as a whole. That is how, according to Hegel, the
state and the bureaucracy inseparable from it become
"actualized." Although bureaucracy presupposes the existence of special groups, it is led to struggle against
them in the course of defending its own interests. Let us
now suppose that as a result of over-all processes of
growth organic bonds have begun to form between the
various partial groups, and that society seeks to abolish
the corporative structure which impedes its development. If this takes place, the bureaucracy will work very
hard to preserve this structure. Why? Because the bureaucracy, a civil society within the political society, the
state, would crumble away if the corporative structure,
i.e., a state within civil society, were eliminated. From
this situation derive the complex tactics and strategy of
the bureaucrats. The crumbling away of the civil society
within the political society (i.e., the bureaucracy) and
of the political society within the civil society (the corporations and the corporative spirit) would mark "the
end of spiritualism and its opposite, materialism."[67]
Philosophical representations and political representation would lose their foundation, their reason for existence. Philosophy, with its ideological corollaries and
implications, would disappear.

The definitive rationality Hegel ascribes to society

and the state turns out to be peculiarly limited, "spirit" rather than reason, a metaphysical transposition, an absolutizing of the actually existing limitations which impede progress. In a society whose highest expression is the state, the limitations are experienced as transcendent in philosophy, religion, and other manifestations of the "spirit"—the same spirit which creates corporations within society and the bureaucracy within the state. The corporative spirit and the bureaucratic spirit are occasionally in conflict, but form a defensive alliance whenever their existence is threatened by a movement of society as a whole.

Bureaucracy is a form, then, the form of a society dominated by the state, the actual content of which Hegel does not discuss, confining himself to the form of bureaucracy and asserting its rationality. Bureaucracy has this particular feature, that it tends to separate itself from its own content. It does not confine itself to formally organizing, to imposing its own form on, that content. It becomes a "formalism," and *qua* formalism it presents itself as superior "consciousness," "the will of the state," the actual state power. Thus a particular interest (bureaucracy's own) lays claim to universality while the general interest is reduced thereby to the status of a special interest. The bureaucracy, the apparatus of the state, profits from the very confusion it creates and feeds. It protects "the imaginary universality of the special interest,"[68] namely, its own spirit. The bureaucracy recognizes the components of civil society only at this fictitious level. This clever transposition may be successful, for although each particular component turns its special interest against the bureaucracy, it accepts the bureaucracy and even supports it, using it as a weapon against the other particular components and special interests. As a result, "The bureaucracy *qua* the perfect corporation is victorious over the corporation *qua* imperfect bureaucracy."[69] It reduces the corporations to a mere appearance, but it wants this appearance to exist and to believe in its own existence in order to preserve its own conditions of existence as mere conditions (subordinate to it). Consequently, while every corporation tends to form a kind of little state within civil society, the bureaucracy is nothing but the state transmuted into a kind of civil (i.e., nonpolitical) society.

In the course of this transmutation, state formalism, i.e., the state *qua* formalism, becomes a reality. It constitutes itself as actual power, it gives itself a content. This means that the bureaucracy is a tissue of *practical* illusions. It is a sort of praxis but one shot through with illusions about itself, its place in the whole, its importance, and its competence. Realities, fictions, illusions are all mixed up together in the actual exercise of its functions. The bureaucracy embodies and furthers the illusion that the state is indispensable and rational. "The bureaucratic spirit is entirely Jesuitic, theological. The bureaucrats are the Jesuits and theologians of politics. The bureaucracy is *la république prêtre*."[70]

Once again analysis obliges us to reject Hegel's identification of the real and the rational, Being and knowing (or consciousness). Seen in its actual density, reality turns out to be full of gaps and disguises woven out of actually experienced illusions and illusions born of illusion. The state bureaucracy embodies a certain rationality, but it is an incomplete, deceptive, and even mendacious rationality. That it seems to be complete and definitive, that it usurps rights and powers which could belong only to an organically unified society which has overcome its contradictions—these facts are part of the illusions, deceptions, and lies. The very need for an ideology (a systematized philosophic representation) to conceal the gaps and disguises of the bureaucratic system shows that this bureaucratic-political construction has no rational necessity whatever.

What consequences may be traced from the fact that bureaucracy, the embodiment of the state spirit, has interests and objectives of its own, distinct from those of the state?

The bureaucracy sets its goal and its spirit against those of the state, some of the time if not all the time. *Qua* formal spirit of the state, it finds that the state is actually devoid of spirit; in trying to supply this lack it conceives of its mission as a formal duty, a categorical imperative in the Kantian sense. Its efforts to amend the state only confirm its belief that it is the goal and the supreme meaning of the state. A confusion and inversion similar to those we noted between the bureaucracy and the component sections of the body politic now characterize the relations between the state and "its" bureaucracy. The confusion and inversion involved are those between form and content. Magically, the bureaucracy changes pure form into concrete content, content into form, formal goal into practical activity. The goals of the state change into goals of the bureaucracy, and vice versa; the inextricable tangle does not preclude conflicts. "The bureaucracy is a circle from which no one can escape."[71] But the metaphor of the magic circle is misleading. This circle, too, is a hierarchy of circles, the lower ones determining the others (Marx in this passage seems to have been thinking of Dante's hell). This hierarchy is built upon and justified by "knowledge" or know-how.

Let us examine this bureaucratic "knowledge," then, the scope of the offices and the competence of the experts who run them. This knowledge has several distinctive features. It constitutes or seeks to constitute a coherent whole, a system. This systematic character, confirmed by philosophy, is supposed to guarantee the veracity of the bureaucrats, to make the bureaucracy the criterion of truth, ruling out illusions and appearances. It cannot resist criticism. To begin with, the system of knowledge is itself expressed as a hierarchy of knowledge. The head knows more than the lower limbs but relies on them in matters of detail. The lower limbs, meanwhile, believe the head is perfectly capable of a rational grasp of the over-all situation. In this way they delude each other. Knowledge is split into working details on the one hand, over-all issues on the other, the empirical and the rational, reality and illusion, the material and the spiritual. Just as in philosophy! All that is known or believed to be known is split in two. Every thing takes on two meanings: one real and practical, the other bureaucratic (in, by, for the bureaucracy). An allegedly comprehensive, systematized, coherent knowledge is broken up, as in philosophy: into a positivist strain on the one hand, and a voluntarist strain on the other. But in the bureaucratic treatment of men and things, where we are dealing with acts, powers, wills, the situation is more serious than in philosophy. In this inverted world, real beings are treated according to their bureaucratic being, according to the image the world of bureaucracy forms of them. Unreal, transposed meaning actually does take the place of real meaning, spirituality the place of materiality. The bureaucracy reserves to it-self the rationality condensed in the social world, sets up a monopoly over it, and the consequence is that ration-ality is changed into its opposite. The irrational situation is revealed by the split in bureaucratic knowledge and by its unreality (or unrealism).

Another split is even more serious. Knowledge is metamorphosed into secrecy, know-how into mystery. The bureaucratic spirit is characterized by the secrecy with which its actual operations are surrounded: within the system the higher functionaries do not reveal their secrets to their subordinates, and the closed character of the bureaucracy as a corporate body protects its secrets from the view of outsiders. Again, the situation is analo-gous to that obtaining in religion, philosophy, and all other ideologies. In all these ways the bureaucracy captures and holds the substance of the state. It stands between the state and public opinion to prevent profana-tion of the state, the supreme spirit, crown on the bu-reaucratic pyramid. What, then, is the actual principle of this so-called "knowledge" or "know-how"? Authority. The worship of authority constitutes the bureaucratic mentality par excellence, in this respect contradicting any system of knowledge. Ideology undergoes a correla-tive transformation. Spiritualism, the idealized represen-tation of the "higher" spheres of reality, the illusory representation of real being, becomes "crude material-ism": the materialism of passive obedience, blind faith, fixed, mechanical, routine duties. To the bureaucra-tized individual, the "higher" goals of the state become his private goal, the pretext for his career. Because his existence is the existence of his particular branch of bureaucracy, the state exists for him only in one frozen form: the only bond between bureaucratic minds is passive obedience to the next higher rank in the hierarchy. Real knowledge becomes empty; real life appears only as dead, since the false knowledge and imaginary life of the working bureaucracy at its various levels are mistaken for the truth.

Though the bureaucracy changes its ideology to one of crass materialism, it nonetheless clings to a crude spiritualism, its dangerous idealism. It wants to "take care of everything." It tends to make will, its own will, the first cause, the absolute. The bureaucrat feels the need to prove his existence by what he does: to him the whole world becomes "something to work on."

Marx's radical criticism uncovers the social truth contained in Hegel's philosophico-political approach to the state. Hegel treats bureaucracy as an essence, an embodiment of the Idea. But this essence, this Idea incarnate, turns out to be full of contradictions, like the Hegelian system as a whole, like philosophy and ideology generally. Hegel makes use of empirical data relative to the Prussian state and the modern state in general, treating them by the method of formal logic. He subsumes them under a general category, ignoring their specific features. By doing this he gives the lie to his own dialectical method. Instead of formulating the logic of political bodies, he simply introduces a political body into his fantastic logic, thereby making it an integral part of his philosophico-political system.

He gets into a tangle every time he comes to grip with a specific problem, for instance, that of the administrative relations between the various components of civil society and the government. Are the administrators to be elected or to be appointed by the authorities? Hegel suggests a mixture—election plus investiture by the government. This hybrid solution reflects the duality of the Hegelian system as a whole.

Hegel seems unaware of the actual mechanism of the state he includes in his system. He does not discuss the functioning of the courts, the police, or the representative bodies. In actual fact, because the state is alien to, outside and above civil society, the delegates and representatives it appoints or approves take its side *against* civil society. The police, the courts, the civil service do not act in the interests of civil society, they are state agencies which serve the interests of the state first and foremost.

We hardly need to show that Marx's radical criticism of political philosophy, the state, and bureaucracy (a criticism accompanying a sociological analysis of these rational irrationalities) implies the objective of revolutionary praxis, namely, democratic self-management, without bureaucracy or state. Bureaucracy can be dispensed with when the general interest becomes in fact—not fictitiously, not at the level of speculative abstraction—identical with the particular interests, and this cannot come about until the particular interest is actually raised to the level of the general interest, the interest common to all "estates," to the whole of civil society. This is the conclusion to which we are led by Marx's analysis—a conclusion of capital importance: for it is the first definition of "communism."

Such is the organic unity to be achieved, marking a higher stage than political democracy (i.e., than the democratic state viewed as a political system).

It is true that to Hegel (and to bureaucracy) society as it is is already rational, and even democratic in a way: after all, every citizen can become an official. According to Hegel, this guarantees the identity between political and civil society, between the state and the bureaucracy on the one hand, and the citizenship on the other. Similarly, Marx ironizes, every Catholic can become a priest, and every soldier can desert and join the enemy.[72]

The bureaucratic system of "knowledge" is expressed on the practical plane by a system of competitive examinations on the basis of which officials are recruited. If the Hegelian state were really rational, examinations to become a cobbler would make more sense. In actual fact, in this allegedly rational state, examinations are a formality: they mark the recognition of bureaucratic knowledge as the privilege of a kind of freemasonry. Examinations do not reflect an objective bond between the individual and the government, do not express their unity; rather, they stress the need for a dual knowledge—one required for life in civil society, and one required for life in the state. "The examination is merely a baptism into bureaucratic knowledge, official recognition of the transubstantiation of secular into sacred knowledge,"[73] of empirical and practical knowledge gained by experience of working and the division of labor into the knowledge possessed by the bureaucracy and the state, a mixture of competence and secrecy.

The Hegelian theory of the state becomes slightly comical when the philosopher "deduces" the salaries paid to officials: the job demands sacrifices; it imposes on one the feeling of duty; the state is secure only if it has an ethics of public office. But the office necessarily becomes just another occupation. An occupation presupposes a salary, and hence it is the government official's salary, not the ethics, which secures the stability of modern societies!

The philosopher becomes positively disquieting when he asserts that "The security of the state and its subjects against the misuse of power by ministers and their officials lies directly in their hierarchical organization and their answerability; but it lies too in the authority given to societies and corporations, because in itself this is a barrier against the intrusion of subjective caprice into the power entrusted to a civil servant, and it completes from below the state control which does not reach down as far as the conduct of individuals."[74]

True, Marx replies, the bureaucrat is tied hand and foot, but even though he is a hammer in relation to those below him and an anvil in relation to those above him, this can hardly reassure anyone. For, Marx asks, "What will protect us against the hierarchy? The lesser evil is to be eliminated by the greater evil."[75] It is also true, Marx goes on to say, that the "conflict, the unresolved conflict between the bureaucracy and the corporations," the fact that civil society, the "estates," can oppose the state and its bureaucracy—"therein lies the security." But Marx is rather skeptical about the official's "humane demeanor," which, according to Hegel, is a "mental counterpoise" to the mechanical activity involved in acquiring administrative knowledge, business training, and in the actual work done. However, as Marx observes, his job is the official's "substance," his daily bread. With his "moral counterpoise" the official's humaneness is supposed to protect him against himself. "What a unity!" exclaims Marx. "Mental counterpoise! What a dualist category!" Hegel, he adds, describes the bureaucratic spirit more accurately when he uses such terms as "business routine" and "the horizon of a restricted sphere."[76]

Sociological analysis of bureaucracy leads to an indictment of every bureaucracy, especially every government bureaucracy. Bureaucratic rationality is not to be taken at its face value, still less regarded as an absolute. But Marx's criticism of bureaucracy is inseparable from his criticism of philosophy and the state.

It might be objected that with this radical criticism of the state and its social foundation, the bureaucracy, Marx rejects Hegel's thesis that there is a rationality inherent in society. This might be seen as leading to a kind of anarchism or a return to voluntarism, for it implies the destruction of the machinery of the state and the dismemberment of the social body. Then, instead of recognizing with the overwhelming majority of theorists, sociologists, historians, and economists that society is organic and rational, we would, like the anarchists, be obliged to ascribe to it a fundamental and unconditional spontaneity or assume that it is organized by a rational higher will.

The answer to these objections can be found in a letter from Marx to Ruge, dated September 23, 1843. The state expresses a certain rationality, but at a given stage of historical and social development, the rationality produced by this development requires the disappearance of the state. Not only is the real not identical with the rational: it may happen that the real is the opposite of the rational. With capitalism, with the state, we are living in an "inverted world," where the most real element, the social, is regarded as the least real (as less real than the political), where the first (the producers) are the last, and the last (middlemen of all kinds) are regarded as creators, and where actual conditions are ignored. The only way to change this state of affairs is to make the world and society more rational, to restore the true unity of the real and the rational by synthesizing them in a higher unity.

"Reason has always existed," Marx wrote in his letter to Ruge, "but not always in rational form. The critic thus can take his point of departure from any form of theoretical or practical knowledge, and on the basis of specific aspects of reality formulate the true reality as the ultimate goal to be achieved. As for real life, precisely the modern political state, even where not consciously inspired by socialist ideas, nonetheless reflects the demands of reason."[77]

Thus a certain rationality is inherent in the state, in the way it functions, and in how it is organized. Everywhere it presupposes reason, but this is only realized up to a certain point. Wherever a state exists, it lays claim to be the embodiment of reason, and in a sense is such an embodiment in respect of its organizations, technicians, administrators, right down to its policemen. But at the same time it everywhere discloses a contradiction between its theoretical definition and actual presuppositions. There is no state without an internal conflict, that is to say, the state bears the seeds of its own destruction. Consequently, the social truth can be elicited everywhere. Just as religion is the compendium of mankind's theoretical struggles, so the political state is the compendium of mankind's practical struggles. In its form the political state expresses all the actual social struggles, social needs, and social truths *sub specie rei publicae.*

Although ultimately the state must be transformed

or abolished, it is essential to choose the proper means to this end. The state must be scrutinized closely as a compendium of *social* needs, *social* struggles, *social* truths. Criticism from the state must start from the fact that it contains a truth, though in disguised, concealed form, and theoretical analysis lays bare this truth. There is social truth in politics just as there is social truth in philosophy.

> "In the course of its development, the working class will replace civil society with an association which will abolish classes and their antagonisms. There will no longer be political power in the strict sense, for political power is merely the official résumé of the antagonism within civil society."[78]

Marx's critical analysis of bureaucracy might suggest that he had made a close study of the institutions and constitutions of the various states. This was not the case. He is not concerned with the state in itself but with the relations between society and the state. His political analysis does not essentially deal with "the political situation" within the state (a matter of tactics) but with the situation of the state within society. As he sees it, political sociology is a political act. Why, then, bother to study such and such a state in itself, as a thing apart?

It must be noted that in discussing the relations between society and the state Marx had the example of England in mind, then the leading industrial country, where the state was not interfering too much with social development or the democratic process, and the proletariat was forging ahead slowly but without encountering insurmountable obstacles. It was clear to Marx that no state, even one founded on brute force (for instance, on conquest), could survive unless it had a social foundation and performed indispensable functions.

"In order to defend the common interests, society created special organisms, originally by simple division of labor. These organisms, the highest of which is state authority, eventually began to serve their own interests, and gradually the servants of society became its masters."

This was how Marx characterized the state after the Paris Commune when he declared that as a result of it, "The struggle of the working class against the capitalist class and its state has entered a new phase." Although the state is born of the social division of labor, it ends up setting itself above society.

That France has just such a state is only too obvious:

"This executive power, with its enormous bureaucratic and military organization, with its ingenious state machinery, with a host of officials numbering half a million, besides an army of another half million, this appalling parasitic body, which enmeshes the body of French society like a net and chokes all its pores, sprang up in the days of the absolute monarchy with the decay of the feudal system which it helped to hasten. The seigniorial privileges of the landowners and towns were transformed into so many attributes of the state power, the feudal dignitaries into paid officials, and the motley pattern of conflicting medieval plenary powers into the regulated plan of a state authority whose work is divided and centralized as in a factory. The first French revolution with its task of breaking all separate local, territorial, municipal, and provincial powers, in order to create the civil unity of the nation, was bound to develop what the absolute monarchy had begun: centralization, but at the same time the extent, the attributes, and the agents of governmental power. Napoleon perfected this state machinery. The Legitimist monarchy and the July monarchy added nothing but a greater division of labor, growing in the same measure as the division of labor within bourgeois society created new groups of interest, and hence new material for state administration. Every *common* interest was straightway severed from society, counterposed to it as a higher, *general* interest, snatched from the activity of society's members themselves and made an object of government activity, from a bridge, a schoolhouse, and the communal property of a village community to the railways, the national wealth, and the national university of France."

Upon what foundation was this vast structure built, which successive revolutions (1789/93, 1830, 1848) perfected instead of demolishing, and which the various parties struggling for power looked upon as the spoils rightfully belonging to the victor? Why, upon the most populous class in French society—the small-holding peasants. They form an enormous mass, "the members of which live in similar conditions, but without entering into manifold relations with one another. Their mode of production isolates them from one another instead of bringing them into mutual intercourse."

Every family, every small holding in this class of society, forms a distinct economic and social unit, whose aim is to be self-sufficient.

"A small holding, a peasant and his family, alongside them another small holding, another peasant, another family. A few score of these make up a village, and a few score of villages make up a Department."

The small peasants constitute a class by virtue of their economic condition, and yet, because the bonds among them are merely local, they do not constitute a true class. They are incapable of defending their class interests without help. "They cannot represent themselves, they must be represented. Their representative must at the same time appear as their master, as an authority over them, as an unlimited governmental power."[79]

These passages have been quoted many times and deserve to be quoted again. Every phrase is telling. They show how brilliant polemics and radical criticism can go hand in hand with scientific objectivity. Everything is there: the origin of the state in the division of labor; its political function in conditions of low productivity, i.e., of relative scarcity; its parasitic aspect; how it takes possession of society's substance; and how it assumes the leading position and unites a society composed of scattered, almost autonomous territorial units. As Marx had said in *The German Ideology:* "The real conditions which in no way depend on the will of individuals . . . are not created by the state. On the contrary, it is they that create the latter."[80]

The state always represents a sphere of society that sets itself above society; within this over-all pattern historical variations are observable. What made possible the establishment of the state in Germany between the sixteenth and the nineteenth century was the weakness of the various social classes and strata; in the case of France, it was the weakness of a specific class (the small peasants).

"This weakness of the various particular spheres—
for here [in the case of Germany] we cannot speak of
estates or classes but at best only of declining 'estates'
and classes in process of forming—did not permit any
one of them to achieve exclusive domination. As was
inevitable in the period of absolutism, the particular
sphere which was entrusted with administration gained
abnormal independence, which was carried even farther
in the modern bureaucracy. In this way the state established itself as a seemingly autonomous power."[81]

What Marx calls "abnormal" here is the fact that
society was robbed of its social functions, that social
practice was supplanted by political practice, and that
this situation became consolidated instead of just a
transitory stage to be quickly left behind by the social
development and the practical life of society.

Thus, even though the efforts of the state may be
sometimes sound or fruitful, for instance, in respect of
encouragement to economic growth, the fact remains
that (civil) society lets itself be dispossessed of its own
initiative. Out of weakness or under duress society has
surrendered the task of managing the common interest
to the apparatus of government; the latter runs things in
its own way, under the name of the "general" interest,
subordinating the actual interests of society to the interests of ruling groups and government bodies.

Marx has often been criticized for inconsistency
when he discusses the role of government in the modern
state, sometimes ascribing real and positive functions to
it, sometimes viewing it as a parasitic growth upon the
body social.

In fact, when Marx analyzes "the Asiatic mode of
production," he stresses the efficiency of government in

its economic functions. Only a great administrative body such as the state could carry out irrigation projects, drain swamps, control the course of rivers, etc., and such projects are indispensable to agriculture and trade. The elementary need for water resources to be regulated for the common good induced private entrepreneurs to form associations (in Italy and the Low Countries, for example), whereas in the East state intervention was required, because there the level of civilization was too low and the territories too vast to make possible associations of this kind.

In those vast stretches of territory, peasant communities (agricultural-pastoral or village communities) have remained unchanged for thousands of years. The cities, relatively unproductive islands in the midst of farmland, served as administrative and military centers. The monarch and the agents of his government acquired ownership of the land and appropriated the social surplus product. The state was so important in these Asiatic empires, says Marx, that "agriculture could degenerate under one government and come back to life under another." Such has been the case in Egypt from the earliest times, also in India and China.[82]

It would seem, then, that Marxian thought on this score is, if not inconsistent, at least ambiguous. However, we may observe that this alleged ambiguity has hardly been dispelled today, but merely supplanted by the dogmatism of official Marxists. Some have overlooked "the Asiatic mode of production" entirely, because for various reasons it embarrasses them. Others have schematized history to such a point that we are told we have already passed through the successive stages of Asiatic mode of production, slavery, feudalism, and capitalism. Each is supposed to have been built on the ruins of the preceding stage, after "liquidating" it more or less completely.

The mist of ambiguity is dispelled if we recognize that Marx admitted several possibilities of historical development, did not subscribe to any straight-line dogma. The historical possibilities Europe realized were not exactly paralleled in the history of the other continents (this hypothesis was formulated in the course of the recent discussion). To the extent that history exhibits apparent inconsistencies, i.e., diversities, they are accounted for by the fact that history is richer and more complex than Marxist dogmatism allows.

So far as we are concerned, it has been established that critical analysis of the state in any Marxian sense must be based on specific studies of every known mode of production, every historical phase, every country. And this in terms of both the structural aspect (classes) and the conjunctural aspect (conquests, domination, characteristics of the conquerors and their armies, etc.). Governments reveal the particularities of the society they administer and set themselves above; they sum up, as we have seen, its struggles and conflicts. Conversely, specific sociological and historical studies help us understand governments by taking into account the multiple conditions under which one or another state was formed.

For Marx, just as for Hegel, truth is always concrete, specific, particular (and yet has its place within the whole or totality). However, in this connection as in others, Marx put the Hegelian formulations "back on their feet." The concrete is social, not political.

It is not hard to pick out in Marx's works many concrete analyses worthy of being called "sociological."

We have already cited several. Here is one that is not very well known though it could serve as a model of the kind:

> "The superstition that used to ascribe revolutions to the ugly intentions of agitators is a thing of the past. Today everyone knows that whenever a revolutionary upheaval takes place, its source lies in some social need that outdated institutions are not meeting. The need may not be felt strongly enough or widely enough to obtain immediate success, but any attempt at brutal repression will only make it more powerful. . . . Our task consists in studying the causes of the recent uprising and finding out why it was defeated. . . . The movements of February/March 1848 were not the work of individuals acting on their own, but irresistible spontaneous manifestations of needs. . . ."[83]

This is followed by an analysis of the class situation and social needs in Germany in 1848.

Our brief survey of Marx's political sociology would be incomplete, misleading even, if we stopped here. It would appear a purely speculative, contemplative knowledge, which amounts to saying it is a contradiction in terms: according to Marx, speculation and contemplation bar access to the concrete, and hence to knowledge. Marxian thought is not merely oriented toward action. It is a theory of action, reflection on praxis, i.e., on what is possible, what impossible. Understanding of the state and the bureaucracy of government is inseparable from the revolutionary activity that is trying to go beyond them. We know to what extent knowledge implies radical criticism (the negative "moment") and at the same time underwrites such criticism. Yet the meaning and scope of critical thought is realized only in practical revolutionary action, in deeds not words.

The transition from political criticism to political action raises the closely connected questions: that of the revolutionary movement, and that of its strategy.

In Marx's view the historical process is fundamental, irreplaceable. It is not "inevitable" in a deterministic sense. It is infinitely complex, although it can be broken down into levels, periods, particular and specific histories (of technology, economy, law, philosophy, etc.). Its partial aspects are finite, the fundamental process as such is not: it reflects human experience as a whole, a collection not of factual data, but of their underlying meanings. It leaves room for human choices without being completely controlled. Control of nature and history is an ultimate goal which is never completely achieved. The process of history generates the unforeseen—otherwise no creation would be possible. At the level under discussion, the level of the state, the social forces and the political determinisms that make up the motive forces of history are supplied by the revolutionary movement represented by the working class. Nothing happens in existing societies dominated by the modern state without it. Whether latent or manifest, the pressure of the proletariat causes historical change— once, that is, the proletariat has emerged as a political force (i.e., as soon as it constitutes itself as a social class and exists as such). The pressure may grow stronger or weaker, the rate of change is now slow now fast, depending on the over-all historical situation and the sociopolitical structures within the different countries. It cannot stop.

In the past, changes in the techniques and modes of

production were, whether directly or indirectly, *causes* of social transformations. Class struggles, reflected in ideologies, provided the *reasons* for the transformations. With the advent of the proletariat, causes and reasons are to be brought together, to the point of fusing in a higher social rationality. This implies a qualitative leap, class contradictions disappearing in the new unity, though the classes themselves do not vanish literally overnight. Consequently, according to Marx, the process of history is not the same thing as Hegel's "Becoming," a winding road that builds itself, defines itself, and creates its own future by perpetually turning back upon itself. So speculative a determination is no longer sufficient. The process of history seeks itself and proves itself in praxis. Its "subject" is not the Mind becoming conscious of itself, not Hegel's Absolute Spirit. The subject, rather —if we may still use this philosophical term—is the working class. As such it is an object of sociological study.

The process of history so conceived has two aspects already mentioned yet which cannot be stressed enough: a qualitative and a quantitative aspect. The quantitative aspect refers to economic *growth* (technological improvements, increases in material production, expressed in tons of wheat, steel, etc.). The qualitative aspect refers to social *development* (intensity of social life, the efficacy of organizations that replace the political with the social element in the process of going beyond democracy, the production of "spiritual" works). These two aspects, though never completely separate, do not necessarily go hand in hand. Quantitative growth (the forces of production) may unfold gradually over a certain period and only later be followed by a qualitative leap forward. Economic growth is possible without the intervention of the working class, social development is not.

The revolutionary movement seeks its way and forges ahead. It is the task of theory to clear this way, to see to it that the movement does not bog down or commit costly errors. The movement is not infallible. It proves itself by advancing, but the advance is often tentative and not always victorious. It encounters obstacles. Political theory is the theory of this movement, for the movement needs a theory. The need is social: theory and practice are inseparable. Theory unfolds with the practice, but the unity between them is not determined in advance, is not always the same; it is not empirical or logical, but dialectical. At critical moments in history there may even be conflicts between theory and practice.

What form, then, should theory take? That of a program or that of a strategy?

Marx does not seem entirely to have rejected the idea of a program. However, he did not believe it has the miraculous property of stimulating or furthering the movement when the latter wavers, marks time, or retreats. "One step forward is more important than a dozen programs."[84]

As for the general concept of strategy, it has been elaborated in our own time (in mathematics, sociology, history), and so postdates Marx. However, it had already been formulated by Clausewitz who, it may be interesting to recall, was inspired by Hegel. Lenin studied Clausewitz for a better understanding of warfare and its bearing upon the revolutionary movement.

We can thus bring up the concept of political strategy, although Marx never explicitly referred to it or employed it in methodical fashion. We know how such concepts are formed. The best example is the concept of social labor. It was derived from praxis under well-defined conditions at the close of the eighteenth century. As the division of labor got more advanced, it became necessary to conceptualize the unity underlying the various types of labor—what they have in common—in society viewed as a whole. Continuing technological improvements, moreover, including the introduction of automated machines in industry, have opened up the prospect of manual labor being one day outmoded entirely. The concept of social labor was elaborated at the economic level by economists (Adam Smith, Ricardo, and Marx himself). Later it reacted, as it were, on history; thanks to it we began to understand how societies which did not have this concept worked and produced, and how their activities were reflected ideologically. We may suppose that something similar applies to the concept of strategy. Long before the concept was formulated, there had been military and political strategies. Machiavelli first formulated the concept; Clausewitz elaborated it. Since then it has been refined (in games theory, operational and symbolic logic, etc.). It leads us to look differently at the past.

Many passages in Marx's writings reflect concern with the political strategy of the working class movement. Use of the term "strategy" is justified in this connection provided we bear in mind that to Marx, (1) the objective that determines every tactical move is the strengthening of the international working class movement, and (2) the ultimate political goal of the movement is the abolition of politics—the withering away of the state once its functions have been taken over by society. The second point is of major importance. To leave it out of consideration is to make Marx a Machiavellian (or Machiavelli a precursor of Marx), to view politics or the state as an eternal, supratemporal essence.

We know that for a long time after the 1848 revolution Marx looked upon Russia as the main enemy of the workers' movement. He repeatedly referred to the tsar and his autocratic government as "the policeman of Europe," the watchdog of private property, and maintained that the regime would collapse if a vigorously conducted war were waged against him. During the Crimean war he sharply criticized Palmerston, the British minister, for merely trying to keep the tsar out of the Balkan peninsula but otherwise sparing him. Similarly, in 1870 Marx was anti-French because Napoleon III's policy was directed against German unification. However, on September 4, 1870, his attitude changed abruptly because German unification under Bismarck was now threatening the French republic. In each case his position was determined by what he thought was in the best interests of the movement. It is only too easy to impute to Marx and his political sociology inconsistencies, contradictions, anti-French, anti-German, anti-English positions, etc., once the distinction between strategy and tactics is lost sight of.

In his political writings Marx displayed extraordinary brilliance and vigor. These pieces of political analysis achieve real style. They are often dismissed as purely occasional pieces, their theoretical importance and the light they cast on his personality neglected. Here is a sample of "concrete political sociology," Marx's portrait of Palmerston:

"Although a septuagenarian who, since 1807, has occupied the public stage almost without interruption, he continued to remain a novelty, and to evoke all the hopes that use to center upon untried and promising youth. With one foot in the grave, he is supposed not to have begun his true career. If he were to die tomorrow all England would be surprised to learn that he had been Secretary of State for half a century.

"If not a good statesman of all work, he is a good actor of all work. He succeeds in the comic as in the heroic, in pathos as in familiarity, in tragedy as in farce, although the latter may be more congenial to his feelings. He is not a first-class orator, but an accomplished debater. Possessed of a wonderful memory, of·great experience, of consummate tact, of never-failing presence of mind, of gentleman-like variety of talent, of the most minute knowledge of parliamentary tricks, intrigues, parties, and men, he handles difficult cases in an admirable manner, and with a pleasant volatility, sticking to the prejudices and the susceptibilities of his audience, secured from any surprise by his cynic impudence, from any self-confession by his selfish dexterity, and from running into a passion by his profound frivolity, his perfect indifference, and his aristocratic contempt. Being an exceedingly happy joker, he ingratiates himself with everybody. Never losing his temper, he imposes on passionate antagonists. If unable to master a subject, he knows how to play with it. If wanting general views, he is always ready to weave a web of elegant generalities.

"Endowed with a restless and indefatigable spirit, he abhors inactivity, and pines for agitation if not for action. . . . What he aims at is not the substance but the mere appearance of success. If he can do nothing, he will divine anything. Where he dares not interfere, he intermeddles. When unable to vie with a strong enemy, he extemporizes a weak one. Being no man of deep designs, pondering on no combinations of long standing, pursuing no great object, he embarks on difficulties with a view to disentangle himself from them in a showy manner. He wants complications, and when he finds them not ready, he will create them. He exults in show-conflicts, show-battles, show-enquiries, diplomatic notes to be exchanged, ships to be ordered to sail, all ending in violent parliamentary debates, which are sure to prepare for him an ephemeral success—the constant and exclusive object of all his exertions. He manages international conflicts like an artist, driving matters to a certain point, retreating when they threaten to become serious, but having got, at all events, the dramatic excitement he desires. The history of the world is, in his eyes, a pastime, expressly invented for the noble Viscount Palmerston of Palmerston. . . .

"Yielding to foreign influence in fact, he opposes it in words. Having inherited from Canning England's mission of propagating Constitutionalism on the continent, he never lacks a theme to pique the national prejudices, so as to counteract revolution abroad and, at the same time, to keep awake the suspicious jealousy of foreign powers. . . . Although a Tory by origin, he introduced into the management of foreign affairs all the shams that form the essence of Whiggism. He knows how to conciliate a large phraseology with narrow views, how to clothe the policy of a peace-mongering middle-class in the haughty language of England's aristocratic past, how to appear an aggressor where he yields, and a defender where he betrays, how to manage his apparent enemy, and how to exasperate his pretended ally, how to find himself at the opportune moment on the side of the stronger against the weak, and how to utter brave words in the act of running away. . . .

"If he has betrayed foreign peoples, he did it with great politeness, politeness being the small coin of the devil, which he gives in change for the life-blood of his dupes. If the oppressors were always sure of his active support, the oppressed never lacked a great ostentation of his rhetorical generosity. . . . At all events, it has been till now a probable chance of success to have him for one's adversary, and a sure chance of ruin to have him for a friend. But, if his art of diplomacy does not shine in the actual results of his foreign negotiations, it shines the more brilliantly in the construction he has induced the English people to lay upon them, by accepting phrases for facts. . . . Excepting the intervals of Tory administration from November 1834 till April 1835, and from 1841 to 1846, he is responsible for the whole foreign policy of England from the revolution of 1830 till December 1851. . . .

"His debut in parliamentary life was of a no less characteristic sort. On February 3, 1808 he rose to defend—what? Secrecy of diplomatic negotiations. . . ."[85]

How could anyone claim that Marx was solely concerned with abstractions, over-all "historical determinisms," and failed to see individuals because of exclusive interest in the "masses," etc.?

Without going into detail, let us try to bring out the main lines of Marx's political strategy, as implied in his sociological discussions and political analyses. In our opinion, he envisages three strategies for the revolutionary movement, i.e., three distinct sets of historical possibilities:

1 The movement rallies a majority of the "people," and, without recourse to violence, seizes power to realize its economic and social objectives.

2 The movement rallies a majority of the "people," but has to fight the ruling classes to get control of the economic and political resources.

3 The movement can rally only a minority of the "people," but this minority proves sufficiently energetic, heroic, and agreed upon common aims to give battle to the ruling classes.

The term "people" as used here has a restricted meaning: it denotes various social strata—peasants, craftsmen, traders, intellectuals, liberal bourgeois—grouped around a proletarian hard core, and tactically allied with it. In other words, it has specific political meaning, but its sociological meaning is vague.

The first strategy applied to England at the time Marx was living there. The situation was that of a political democracy constantly being extended to more and more of the population through universal suffrage and thus—under pressure from a powerful, well-organized working class—in a position to go beyond that situation, asserting its political hegemony in a gradualist fashion, without recourse to armed insurrection. In such a situation, the goal can be attained through economic and social reform, but the strategy is meaningful and promising only if pursued with an energy that would, if necessary, rise to the strategy of revolution, explicitly preparing for the possibility.

"Someday the workers must conquer political supremacy in order to establish the new organization of labor; they must overthrow the old political system whereby the old institutions are sustained. . . . Of course, I must not be supposed to imply that the means to this end will be everywhere the same. . . . There are certain countries, such as the United States and England, in which the workers may hope to secure their ends by peaceful means."[86]

The second strategy corresponded to the situation in Germany, where national unity had been imposed "from above," where the feudal landowners (a squire-archy) still held strong positions, and where collusion between them and the bourgeoisie was of long standing. The failure of the 1848 revolution had made this situation clear to all. Had the outcome of this revolution been different, gradual transformation of the society through political reform might have been possible: the achievement of unification could have touched it off. But Bismarckism, the German variation on Bonapartism, surely reduced the chances of such a development:

> "The working class in Germany is, in its social and political development, as far behind that of England and France as the German bourgeoisie is behind the bourgeoisie of those countries. Like master, like man. The evolution of the conditions of existence for a numerous, strong, concentrated, and intelligent proletarian class goes hand in hand with the development of the conditions of existence for a numerous, wealthy, concentrated, and powerful middle class. The working class movement itself never is independent. . . ."[87]

The third strategy was represented by the situation in France. The democratic bourgeois revolution of 1789 was led by urban minorities which carried part of the peasants along with them, neutralized another part, and had to fight a third section of the peasantry as well as the upper-class carryovers from feudalism. The party of the socialist proletarian revolution need not follow in the footsteps of the Jacobins and the Blanquists. But Jacobinism and Blanquism, which succeeded the revolution of 1789, are specifically French historical facts, and the new party must take them into account, as well as the tendency to anarchism, which also revolves around a tradition of "activist minorities." The experiences of 1848 and 1871 confirm this assessment.

Thus every conceivable (nineteenth-century) situation was envisaged by the new party's strategy. This was the basis for the expression "the permanent revolution." When Marx used it—we have already noted that it did not come readily to his pen—it did not mean what it came to mean later: a policy of continuous violence, constant and unremitting attack by any and every means. It did to Marx denote an unceasing struggle, but one that passes through various phases each requiring an appropriate strategy and tactics. It calls for the boldest, most radical solutions to each successive problem, each historical conflict. It points to the period of transition—between the destruction of the existing state and the setting up of a state that will wither away:

> "The proletariat rallies more and more round revolutionary Socialism, round Communism, for which the bourgeoisie has invented the name of Blanqui. This socialism is the declaration of the permanence of the revolution, the class dictatorship of the proletariat as the necessary transit point to the abolition of class distinctions generally, to the abolition of all the relations of production on which they rest."[88]

The criteria for deciding upon one strategy rather than another are: analysis of the social structure (classes and fractions of classes), evaluation of the tactical opportunities available at a given moment, and critical study of the government in power. When the ruling classes have a powerful bureaucratic and military establishment, the odds are that revolutionary violence will be touched off and that the movement will be obliged to resort to an armed uprising. Gradual transition to socialism by way of political, economic, and social reforms seems possible to Marx only where the state *qua* instrument of the ruling classes is undermined by internal contradictions.

Questions concerning the nature of the movement and the strategy to be followed lead us to another important question—that of the nation. How seriously are the facts of nationality and the system of nation-states to be taken?

In his writings Marx frequently discussed specific national situations, but he treated them at the level of strategy rather than general theory. He seems to have believed that even in his day the workers' movement had transcended national boundaries. Although the world market created by capitalism has cleared the way toward abolition of national boundaries, "The bourgeoisie has its particular interests in each country," he wrote, "and since its interests are its supreme value, it cannot transcend nationality."

On the other hand, the proletarians of every country have "one and the same interest, one enemy, one struggle; the proletarians are already for the most part exempt from nationalist prejudice; their movements are essentially humanitarian, anti-national. The proletarians alone can abolish nationality."

These texts dating from 1846 only too clearly reveal what high hopes Marx pinned on the movement shortly before the revolutions of 1848. Nationality, he seems to think, is already a thing of the past. In the same period Marx and Engels were setting up "Correspondence

Committees" in various European countries, which fore-shadowed the foundation of the International. One of the stated aims of these committees was "to get rid of the boundaries of nationality."[89]

However, when analyzing specific problems of political strategy and tactics, considering an alliance or a program, Marx views the nation as the framework within which revolutionary activity is conducted:

> "The Communists are reproached with striving to abolish countries and nationality. The workers have no country. We cannot take from them what they have not got. Since the proletariat must first of all acquire political supremacy, must rise to be the leading class of the nation, must constitute itself *the* nation, it is, so far, itself national, though not in the bourgeois sense of the word. National differences and antagonisms between peoples are vanishing gradually from day to day, owing to the development of the bourgeoisie, to freedom of commerce, to the world market, to uniformity in the mode of production and in the conditions of life corresponding thereto. The supremacy of the proletariat will cause them to vanish still faster."

Thus Marx believes that the proletariat will do away with national boundaries, completing a process begun under capitalism.

"To the extent that the exploitation of man by man is abolished, the exploitation of one nation by another will be abolished, too. Hostility between nations will disappear together with class antagonisms within the nation."

Although the struggle waged by the proletariat against the bourgeoisie is not national in respect of content (historical, social, practical), it is national in respect of form (political). This basic thesis is also expressed in Marx's political last will and testament, his *Critique of the Gotha Program.*

Why not admit frankly that to some extent these famous texts are puzzling to us today? The emphasis here laid on form confirms what we have said above. Study of the forms seems to fall under the heading of sociology. And yet these same texts disclose a certain ambiguity. If form is inseparable from content, and theory from practice, ought not the nation-state and nationality be defined, conceptually formulated, clarified theoretically rather than regarded as *already* a thing of the past? When Marx studies modes of production, he believes that it is possible to go beyond them. He starts from this assumption, which implies that socio-economic relations constitute a historical whole subject to radical critical negation, and that revolutionary practice thereby attains a higher theoretical level. Could not, should not the same method be applied in analyzing the concept of nationhood? Marx seems to sidestep the problem, and it is a problem that has become increasingly urgent and important. The sovereign nations and their governments which the workers' movement confronts are capitalist, their ruling classes bourgeois, more or less allied with surviving feudal elements. At the same time every nation has its own special features within the general framework of the capitalist mode of production. What is the relation between the special and the general in this connection? Of course, this is to pose the problem logically, abstractly, and it would seem highly necessary to go on to concrete economic, sociological, and historical analysis. And yet this is just what we don't have, or only just barely. A scattered few references to the uneven rate of development as between one and another capitalist country hardly fills this serious gap in Marxian thought. Are we to conclude that Marx from the outset placed himself on the normative rather than the conceptual theoretical plane? Or should we say that he viewed the question in the light of his assumption that the revolutionary movement transcends national boundaries?

It might also be said that Marx and Engels fought on two fronts: against a certain "Leftism" (which negated nationhood, "purely national" problems, questions dealing with the independence of peoples and their rights to self-determination), and against a "Rightist deviation" whose spokesmen were narrowly nationalistic and considered their own nations as superior to all others, as models for all to imitate.

No doubt. Such assertions are not false. However, they are not relevant to the concepts involved, only to the strategy or even the internal tactics of the movement. Is this to downgrade or upgrade Marxian theory? That is the question. It would seem that the concepts have failed to provide guidance to the movement, that the movement obeys laws of its own—splits, for instance, into tendencies—Leftism (sectarianism), Rightism (opportunism), Centrism (which gives leeway for maneuvering). Does this mean that practice has come to be set above theory? If this has, in fact, happened, then doesn't theory degenerate into tactical expertise? Isn't this to replace political sociology with a sociology of political tendencies?

On the other hand, these tendencies were less clear-cut in Marx's lifetime than they have been or seem to have been in our own day. Lassalle, though Leftist in one sense (Lassalle's "brazen law of wages"), was also a

German nationalist, an inveterate champion of the Reich. As for the Proudhonian Rightists, they maintained that their ideas on the role of co-operatives, people's banks, etc. were applicable to all countries, and took no note of national peculiarities. In the period of the First International, reformers took a philosophical line rather opposed to nationalism, while extremists were inclined to accept the idea of the nation-state as a fundamental datum of politics. All of which hardly simplifies the problem. . . .

Can we find an answer to our questions in Marx's *Critique of the Gotha Program*, his last major political writing, composed almost thirty years after the *Communist Manifesto* and never intended for publication? The movement had now become a party embodying the hopes and promises of the revolution, and it claimed to be inspired by Marx. Though weakened by illness, Marx was still alive and felt he had to condemn its program. His *Critique* is a solemn warning to the party leaders that their program was not consistent with Marxian theory, both in the sense that their thinking was not scientific and in the sense that their political practice came down to a string of compromises.

What is at issue? The state, the concept of the state, and the related question of nationality, the nation-state as a fact of life. Against whom is Marx fighting? Against the ghost of Lassalle, ten years dead but still haunting the movement. Lassallism, a body of thought very different from Marxism, was having much more influence upon political practice than Marx's own thinking. Lassalle was no theoretician, Marx claimed, he did not *know* what the nature of wages is or what the state really is. He relied on his imagination, his feelings, his impressions. He mixed radical phraseology with a political empiricism that took for granted the existing framework of society, the modern state, and even their governments. Despite real talents, he was a demagogue rather than a revolutionary, who had from the earliest day of the movement managed to steer it along a disastrous course.

Lassalle advocated dubious tactics and strategy dressed up in radical language. When the program stipulates, "In contemporary society the means of labor are the monopoly of the capitalist class," he is eluding the question of land. Such a formulation is only too easy to account for today, Marx observes, alluding to the dealings Lassalle had with Bismarck. Lassalle never attacked the landowners. He did not stop at falsifying the *Communist Manifesto*, though he knew it by heart, so as to cover up the alliance he had made with the feudal elements in Germany against the bourgeoisie. He was a shrewd politician, too shrewd by far.

He had completely failed to grasp the theory of wages and the Marxian concepts of value and surplus value. The program demanded "an equitable distribution of the proceeds of labor." Now, what is an "equitable distribution?" Marx asks. The bourgeois ideologists maintain that it can be achieved, even that it has already been achieved, on the basis of the existing mode of production. Lassalle's "brazen law"—a noble term he borrowed from Goethe, who had spoken of "great brazen laws"—masks the real nature of wages, the social and historical laws governing them, and thereby the future of the workers' struggle. The lofty phrase about equitable distribution of the "proceeds of labor," giving all members of society an equal right in the latter, fails to allow for needs in the transitional period of revolutionary dictatorship. During this period the state has to be destroyed, the means and control of production are to be taken away from the ruling classes, and productive forces are to be increased. What are the "proceeds of labor"? No more or less than the sum total of what society produces. The problem, then, is not at all one of handing over to all workers, still less to all members of society (including those who do no work), the totality of production. Distribution of the national product is governed by laws. It is indispensable to replace outmoded means of production and make investments in order to increase output. A reserve fund must be built up as insurance against natural disasters. The cost of administrative services and of socially indispensable work which is not materially productive, the funds destined for the support of children, the sick, the old, etc., will have to be deducted from the total product.

Such distribution of the national product already takes place in bourgeois society, at once automatically and in line with the interests of the bourgeoisie. In the new society it will be made to operate rationally, according to plan. But it will be some time before it becomes truly equitable. During the transition period, the society that emerges from the old capitalist order will bear its stigmata. The market, production for the market, the law of value, and equivalent exchanges will not disappear for moral reasons, but only once reorganized productive forces have made it possible to go beyond them. Consequently, the "equal right" will remain "equal" in the bourgeois sense, in accordance with the law that governs the exchange of equivalent commodities and contracts. Despite the advances made, i.e., despite the development of society, the rights of the producers will continue to be *proportional* to the quantity and quality of the work performed. Equality will consist solely in this, that everything will be measured by an equal measure, by the labor involved. The "equal" right is an unequal right: it compares and governs unequal labors: "It is therefore a right to inequality, as every right is."

The problem of transition thus reveals the essence of "rights." The theoretical project for a new society, based upon a scientific analysis of reality, is set against the empirical, practical, tactical program. It is formulated at the conceptual level. It elaborates the concept of rights. According to a pattern we are by now familiar with, the emerging concept throws retrospective light over the past. Allegedly equalitarian and rational, the doctrine of rights has always had the function of organizing scarcity, of distributing with seeming equality the products of a basically unequal society. Thus "rights" have a twofold aspect: they give a legal form to inequality, and reflect the pressure of the ruling interests to turn it to their advantage. The concept of rights is thus clarified by the concept of a society that transcends them, and at the same time it throws light on the society ruled by them. Juridical sociology, as we might put it today, cannot be separated from social practice, nor from the idea of going beyond it. Criticism of the concept of rights is part of it. Rights will be left behind only in the higher phase of communist society, when a regime of plenty for all has been achieved.

"Then and only then will it be possible to get out from under the narrow perspectives of bourgeois rights, and society at last will be able to inscribe on its banner: 'From each according to his capacities, to each according to his needs.' "

Rights and the transformations they undergo depend alike on the mode of production, not on advances in the intellectual or moral spheres. Who are those who deny this? "Those who keep popping up with harebrained ideological and juridical schemes—the sort of thing French socialists and democrats are so habituated to."

But now we are coming to the fundamental question, that of the state (and hence that of the modern nation-states as historical phenomena). It is here that Lassalle went completely off the track, or rather conceded too much to his adversaries. He begins with the assertion that, as opposed to the workers, other classes form no more than a "reactionary mass." This formulation, Marx says, is extremist and false. The bourgeoisie itself is revolutionary in relation to the carryovers from feudal society and to those middle strata which cling to a status corresponding to obsolete modes of production. The proletariat is revolutionary in relation to the bourgeoisie, and it alone can bring about the complete transformation of society. Lassalle's deceptive phraseology merely serves as a front for his political projects and reflects a narrowly nationalistic conception of the workers' movement. According to the Gotha program, "The working class strives for its own liberation, first of all, within the framework of the existing national state." Obviously, Marx comments at this point, the working class is to organize as a class in its own country and make that the arena of its struggle. "To this extent its class struggle is purely national, not in content, but in form." Marx harks back to the formulation in the *Manifesto*. He enumerates the difficulties of the situation. The German national state has to be viewed within the framework of the world market and the existing system of states. The bourgeoisie, or the ruling class generally, is perfectly capable of an *international* policy, as was made clear by Bismarck. To fight such a policy, the German working class must take "international functions" upon itself. Otherwise its internationalism falls greatly short of that exhibited by free-trade liberals who also champion peace, freedom, and the brotherhood of peoples.

The trouble with Lassalle was that he supposed you can build a new society the way you build a railway: by borrowing from the government. He had boundless confidence in the state, was thoroughly naive concerning the aid to be expected from it.

In line with Lassalle's ideas the program went on to declare that what the German Workers' Party is striving for is the "free state." This statement, says Marx, is meaningless. It shows how little the German Workers' Party has been affected by socialist ideas. Instead of viewing society as the foundation of the state, the program "treats the state as an independent entity, which possesses its own intellectual and moral foundations, its own freedoms."

We recognize here the same terms in which Marx formulated his criticism of the Hegelian conception of the state. Lassalle, a Hegelian who thought he was a Marxist, failed to understand the nature of the state. Like Hegel, when he describes a given reality and then identifies it with absolute rationality, Lassalle confuses some eternal state (Idea of the state, in Hegel's terms) with the actual state, "which is nothing but a military despotism overlaid with bureaucratic scaffolding, protected by the police, dressed up with parliamentary embellishments and feudal survivals, and already influenced by the bourgeoisie"—namely, the Bismarckian state. Revolutionary objectives are abandoned whenever the term "state" is taken to denote the machinery of government, "the state in so far as it is a special organism resulting from the division of labor." Confused on just this score, the Gotha program merely sought to improve the machinery of government, and kept "within the boundaries of what the police allows, what logic disallows." For all its many fine phrases, it limits itself to demanding democratic control of the existing state by the working people, an income tax, and universal elementary education paid for by the state. The talk about freedom and the free state is idle chatter: from the point of view of political action, freedom consists in "transforming the state, presently an organ set up over society, into an organ entirely subordinated to society."

The formulation is nothing if not clear. In 1875 Marx had not given up any part of his opposition to the state. And he expresses himself more strongly than ever on this score: "Even today, the forms of the state are free precisely to the degree that they restrict the freedom of the state."

The ever-mounting number and size of governmental institutions in modern society call attention as never before to the contradiction between the political and the social aspects. Human freedom has to be defined on the social, not the political plane. Will the modern state manage to stifle social life entirely under the crushing weight of politics? This is the question the Lassallians ignored, but that Marx never tired of raising. And it was against the so-called "realists" that he raised it, those who turn their backs on revolutionary possibilities in the name of "reality," mistake the *status quo* for reality, treating the fundamental concepts of socialism as mere utopianism.

What changes will the form of the state undergo in the new society? What social functions similar to the functions now performed by the state will remain in existence? This question can only be answered "scientifically," i.e., at the conceptual, theoretical level. "It won't be by coupling the word 'People' and the word 'State' in innumerable ways that we will get any closer to solving the problem."

During the transitional period, the people will give the state "a very rough awakening." Political democracy itself will be surmounted, not by improving the state and its democratic, republican institutions, but by destroying both the state as presently set up over society and that portion of society which made such a state possible. The revolutionary dictatorship of the proletariat, the broadening of democracy, the withering of the state are three aspects of one and the same "movement," that of the revolution.

Summing up, in his political last will and testament Marx reaffirms what he has always said about the state and further elaborates one fundamental concept, namely, the concept of revolution. The proletarian revolution implies the end of the state. The internal relation between the two concepts is dialectical—contradiction and unity, a higher synthesis achieved *via* negation, the transitional period. In this period the objective is not simply to destroy the state (that is the anarchist position), but to let society as a whole—the transformed society—take over the functions previously performed by the state. The incomplete rationality inherent in existing society, presently held back because of internal contradictions in the latter, has been taken in charge or, rather, captured by the state. Society must recapture and carry this rationality farther forward, toward its full realization. As it exists presently, the state carries rationality to absurdity.

When he wrote these pages, did Marx think that his warnings would be heeded? If so, by whom? Did he hope that the "movement" would catch up with the theory and its guiding concepts, would cease to lag behind them? Did he believe that the politicians, the bureaucrats, the "realists," the pragmatists would be eliminated from the movement? What did he expect of those to whom his message was addressed, the Bebels, the Liebknechts? What were his long-range objectives? Did he, in his capacity as a theoretician, feel overwhelmed when men of action who did not understand him called themselves Marxists? Was he already aware how weak the movement was getting theoretically—in Germany, where the theoretical level was higher than elsewhere and leaders and working men alike enjoyed thinking themselves the heirs to the great philosophers?

Marx's comments on the Gotha program have lost nothing of their saltiness, and the last of them is an especially odd outburst: *Dixi et salvavi animam meam!* (I have spoken and saved my soul!). Marx had completed his work as theorist and revolutionary. He managed to say what he had to say, had done what he could. The concepts are still with us, as fresh and as enduring as they ever were, the splendid thinking which so many have since judged arid, cold, barren. Marx handed himself over to posterity, to the "movement." What more or else could he have done? No Pontius Pilate he, he does not wash his hands, he never hesitated to speak out. He lived long enough to discern an appalling gulf between self-styled "Marxist" statesmen and his own theory of the state, between practical politicians and practice elucidated by theory. In those last words we detect both hope and fear. Were his last days lived out in bitterness or in peace of conscience? Who can tell?

Conclusion

Our purpose in this book has been twofold:

1 To elucidate some basic Marxian concepts. Marx himself developed them from three principal sources: German philosophy (Hegel), English political economy (Adam Smith, Ricardo), and French socialism (Saint-Simon, Fourier, Proudhon). He did not proceed eclectically or syncretically, but by way of a radical critique of philosophy, political economy, and the socialist "ideal." The conceptions of his precursors were limited by the narrowness of their national and individual outlooks, and we have tried to show how his radical criticism broadened and transcended these conceptions. We have also tried to show where Marx's new concepts originated (praxis, society and social relations, revolution, etc.), and how they can be linked to form a whole by being

raised to a higher level. We have tried to clarify this process and this method. Once the thought inspired by Marx began to lose its critical radicalism, and as positivism or the cult of the positive supplanted the dialectical method of negation and going beyond, these matters were neglected. We have tried to reconstruct Marx's thought in its own movement, in process of forming, keeping close to the texts so as not to "place it in perspective" or "interpret" it.

2 Instead of selecting passages from Marx's writings and relating them to modern conceptions of sociology as a specialized science, we have tried to discern in these writings a sociological method and area of study, without thereby prejudging what other specialized sciences (economy, anthropology, history, psychology, etc.) may be able to draw from the works of Marx. However, we have tried to show in what sense Marx's method implies the project of constituting or reconstituting, exploring or creating a totality (of knowledge, or reality).

It remains for us now to spell out and verify a proposition which has been implicit throughout: Marxian thought is not alone sufficient, but it is indispensable for understanding the present-day world. In our view, it is the starting point for any such understanding, though its basic concepts have to be elaborated, refined, and complemented by other concepts where necessary. It is part of the modern world, an important, original, fruitful, and irreplaceable element in our present-day situation, with particular relevance to one specialized science —sociology.

Let us take this concept of "situation" for granted, as a kind of postulate. Let us suppose there really is such a thing as a theoretical world situation, just as there is an economic or political world situation, and attempt to define it more closely.

According to a view that has been steadily gaining adherents, Marx belongs to the past—not to folklore exactly, but to culture. Which comes nearly to the same thing: after all, is not today's culture yesterday's most advanced thought? Marx, we are told, is representative of an epoch. He was mistaken: his prophecies did not come true. He foretold the end of capitalism, the end of the state, the end of philosophy, the end of human alienation—many, too many "ends." The things he foresaw an end to are still with us, some more firmly established than ever. At the same time, this view holds that Marx's analyses and extrapolations he drew from them express the reality and the hopes of the nineteenth century.

We have already pointed out that Marx predicted the end of competitive capitalism under the double pressure of the proletariat and the monopolies, and that on this score his predictions proved true. Capitalism has indeed survived in one part of the world, and yet it has been transformed. As for so-called capitalist society still dominated (by means other than those employed in Marx's time) by the so-called bourgeoisie, it is just as absurd to say that nothing has changed as to say that nothing has stayed the same. To make out the changes that have occurred and to distinguish them from what has remained stagnant or regressed, do we not have to take Marx's analysis as the basis for such a comparison—namely, the one we find in the work entitled *Capital?*

The adversaries of Marxian thought assert that over the past hundred years a new type of society has emerged, for which the way had been paved long since, and for which Marx himself—despite himself, as it were, despite the revolutionaries he inspired—helped to pave the way. The process that gave birth to this new society is "historical" in the sense that it includes unexpected, unforeseeable elements.

At this point the critics of Marxism part company. Some say, in effect: The process is too vast, too complex for knowledge to encompass and dominate it. Let us give free rein to the forces working toward this new society. The very tensions between them are helpful. All we can do is remove the obstacles standing in their way (these possibly include the action inspired by Marxism, revolutionary efforts consciously to transform the world).

Others say: Let's get the facts straight, make an empirical study of the new world aborning, detail by detail, making use of the specialized sciences. Let's draw upon our vast stores of learning to organize the new society in the light of these sciences, which are defined by their operational efficiency.

We may call the first group the "neo-liberals." There is a good chance that their liberalism conceals a voluntarism. Today no more than yesterday do we have a sure criterion (from the point of view of liberalism) by which to determine obstacles to reason and freedom. Twentieth-century history has made us only too familiar with the divorce between liberal ideology and liberal politics. How often have liberal democrats believed, or pretended to believe, that freedom was being realized because they were in power! How often, while striking out at "the Left," they have left themselves vulnerable on "the Right," with consequences not of any deepening or broadening of democracy but, rather, the sorry spectacle of its dismantling and defeat.

The second group of critics clearly falls under the head of positivism and scientism. We might call them "neo-positivists" or "neo-scienticists." Why "neo"? Because they base themselves on the sciences of man as much as or more than on the sciences of nature. The incomplete, fragmentary character of these sciences does not seem to bother them. They accept a dimming of the image of man. They repudiate "totality"—or sense of the whole—both on the plane of knowledge and on that of human self-realization. They sanction the operational but fragmentary study of social reality. Still, it should be noted that a few recent scientific disciplines—for instance, the theory of information, cybernetics—have "totalizing" ambitions. Neo-positivism puts paid (or so it believes) the intellectual controversy in favor of strictly factual findings. What it studies, what it grasps, is integrated by virtue of being grasped in a system or a structure; science and the scientist are both integrating and integrated parties. This new society into which we are allegedly entering is to be organized, systematized, and hence "totalized." And who is to carry out this task? Needless to say, it will be the state, and within this state, specific groups—the technocrats. Will they succeed? Are they not divided among themselves? Don't they represent divergent interests? Do they not differ according to whether they are active within the public sector of state capitalism or within the sector of "private" capitalism? Don't they introduce new contradictions into society instead of resolving the old ones? Is there perfect agreement between the rationality of the state and that of technology (that of the analytical, operational intellect)? We leave these questions open. One thing sure is that this tendency is giving rise to a diffuse ideology, only as yet partially formulated. Doesn't the exclusive importance ascribed by some to concepts such as those of structure, system, function—which have areas of validity, but which are often misused—reflect this ideology? At least this question makes sense. We would answer it in the affirmative.

Still, we ought to be able to give a name to this new society which is, it seems, being produced by mutation. What shall we call it? There have been a number of suggestions: industrial society, technological society, a consumer society, mass society, the society of leisure, the affluent society, the rational society, etc. Each of these designations has its champions and inspired publications which have enjoyed wide circulation.

Let us take a brief look at each of these hypotheses —for what we have here is hypotheses concerning the essential character of the society engaged in the mutation we are witnessing. Each hypothesis is summed up in a designation that emphasizes a certain feature, and treats it as a definition. This tends to mask the hypothesis implied. Let us try to discover what is true and false in each, what has been established and what is merely extrapolation.

Industrial society? If this means that industrial production gains ever greater preponderance over agricultural production, the term is obviously correct. It must even be acknowledged that Marx was the first (or the second, after Saint-Simon) to stress this fundamental feature of competitive capitalism. Can it serve as basis for an analysis in depth of contemporary society or societies? To think so would be to fall into a narrow "economism" which the Marxian method explicitly rejects. To limit oneself to this designation is to obscure the differences between the various industrial societies, differences stemming from their different histories. Granting that the term "industrial" applies to the type or genus of these societies, the species it includes may differ, and exclusive emphasis on the genus ignores specific differences, particularly those between capitalist society (or societies) and socialist society (or societies). Despite multiple interactions between the two, there can be no doubt that these differences exist and that they will be further accentuated. On the other hand, we must take into account the distinction between economic growth and social development. We have noted how Marx introduced this distinction between the quantitative and the qualitative aspect. In the modern world we witness examples of remarkable, even spectacular growth without development. Marx would not have suspected such a phenomenon, which is the effect of massive state interventions. Social (and "cultural") development can result only from a revolutionary upsurge marked by more flexible institutions, by a deepening of democracy, and an active organizational network "at the base" expressing social needs. Once this aspect of praxis is taken into account, we must willy-nilly go back to the theory of the withering away of the state. Final point: there are only tiny islets of industry in the vast ocean of underdeveloped countries, where agricultural production is still predominant (and will remain so for a long time), supplying the resources for such industrialization as is actually carried out (at very different rates of speed) in the various countries.

A consumer society? It is forgotten that those who control production manufacture their consumers by various means, of which advertising is the most powerful. It is forgotten that this "consumer society" is scarcely concerned at all with social needs, and with individual needs only to the extent that they bring in profits. Supposing it true that elementary needs can today be satisfied, the very existence of higher needs can still be contested, and the evidence for them doubted. There is amazing factualism in their contemporary discussion. The satisfaction of elementary needs in so-called consumer societies seems to be accompanied by a reduction of consumption to the elementary. Moreover, it is not certain that all elementary needs (for instance, housing, education, etc.) are actually being satisfied. The old poverty is being replaced with a new poverty.

The affluent society? Those who launched this designation have shown its limitations. In the United States, they are "discovering" poverty. Sizable minorities (Negroes, recent immigrants, "farmers," etc.) are reported to suffer from low living standards. Waste and the frenzied overconsumption of certain privileged groups cannot conceal the poverty and the "new poverty" far larger groups are suffering from.

The society of leisure? The amount of leisure time has not increased for most people. Though working hours have grown shorter, "forced time" (for instance, time used going back and forth to work) eats up our much-publicized leisure time. People have to keep working to invest; the scale of investment required for automation, for new branches of industry, for the conquest of space, and for aid to backward countries is enormous. This applies to both "socialist" and "capitalist" countries.

The urban society? Yes, near the islets of growth. No, if we take into account the peasants in Africa, Asia, and Latin America. It is no, there, even if we include the Hoovervilles to which uprooted peasants are flocking.

Mass society? As though every society from time immemorial did not rest upon this foundation—the human masses.

A technological society? Predominance of technology does indeed seem to be a fundamental feature of "modern times." It deserves careful consideration. Many persons confuse the speeding up of technological progress with an alleged "acceleration of historical time," with social and cultural development. Whereas a divorce between these aspects of praxis seems no less essential a feature of "modern times." The predominance of technology contributes to the survival if not the salvage of capitalism, in the form of gigantic (monopolistic or state) organizations for promoting technological progress. According to Marx, the bourgeoisie can survive only by continually revolutionizing the conditions of production, lacking which the "revolution" will take over this task! Also, according to Marx, there is a connection, yet at the same time a difference, between man's (technological) *control* over the outside world and his *appropriation* of his own nature, his social existence, his everyday life, his needs and desires. Moreover, technology has only been predominant under one particular set of historical circumstances: where rival socialist and capitalist "armed camps" or "systems" confront one another, under conditions of the armaments race, and the race for conquest of outer space. This set of historical circumstances may, however, become permanent, freeze into a structure. The fact that technology is championed by specific social groups—technologists and bureaucrats, as yet unsuccessful in constituting themselves as a class—

implies certain dangers. The real problem is not to find a definition for the new society, but to elucidate these dangers. Definition, in a sense, tends to conceal the dangers and to present as an accomplished fact what is only a disquieting possibility. To an even greater extent than the other terms for the age, this one ought to inspire radical criticism, i.e., dialectical thought.

It may well be that the present period (of mutation or transition) cannot as yet be given any very exact denomination. Whither are we going? Who can tell? All that is clear is that we're on our way—somewhere. No final end can be assigned despite the fact that there is rationality inherent in this process. Might this not be one of those "flights forward" which drive modern society toward an undeterminable future, toward the possible and the impossible, by way of nuclear terror, the danger of annihilation, and the rational madness of cybernetics?

If we do not want to stop here, contenting ourselves with this vague and endless questioning, we must try to explore the possible and the impossible. How? Starting from Marx. Let us follow the guiding thread: the concept of going beyond philosophy, political economy viewed as a distribution of scarcity, the state, or politics. Then more exact, if not more limited, questions will emerge. Can the socialist countries, which invoke Marx's name so often and claim to be Marxist, bring their praxis closer to the concepts elaborated by Marx, the concepts of revolution and freedom? Can they put an end to the existing gap between ideology and practice? Can the state wither away under socialism as it exists today? Can the social management of society supplant authoritarian planning in these countries? Can the old mortgage be finally paid off? As for the capitalist countries, can "the socialization of society" keep alive and reach maturity within the shell of capitalism, finally bursting it open? In more general terms, can development, by a qualitative leap, catch up with the quantitative growth it is lagging behind in most, if not all, countries of the world today?

All these names for the age conceal ideologies, myths, utopias, in varying proportions. Marxian criticism dispels them. New conflicts are added to the old contradictions and take their place. For instance, there is acute conflict today between the quantitative (growth) and the qualitative (development). It is accompanied by mounting complexity in social relations, which is masked and counteracted by opposed elements. Control over external nature is increasing, while man's appropriation of his own nature is stagnating or regressing. The former falls primarily under the head of growth, the latter of development.

Notes

Notes

[1] *Marx, Sa vie, son oeuvre, avec un exposé de sa philosophie.* Paris, 1964. Cf. pp. 42 ff.

[2] *Contribution to the Critique of Hegel's Philosophy of Right* (1843/44), opening lines.

[3] *Ibid.*

[4] *Differenz der demokritischen und epikureischen Naturphilosophie,* Preface.

[5] The texts which this paragraph sums up may be found in *Marx, Sa vie* etc., and *Oeuvres choisies de Marx,* 2 v. Paris, Gallimard, 1964.

[6] *Ökonomisch-philosophische Manuskripte aus dem Jahre 1844,* in *Marx/Engels Gesamtausgabe,* Marx-Engels-Archiv, Frankfurt, 1927 ff. (henceforth to be referred to as MEGA). First Section, v. III, p. 152.

⁷ Cf. K. Marx, "Aus der Kritik der Hegelschen Rechtsphilosophie," in MEGA, First Section, v. I, pp. 456 ff.

⁸ Letter to Ruge, September 1843. *Ibid.*, p. 572.

⁹ *Die Deutsche Ideologie*, in MEGA, v. V, pp. 15–16.

¹⁰ Cf. *Capital*. Translated by Samuel Moore and Edward Aveling. Chicago, Charles H. Kerr & Co., 1906. v. I, Book I, I, 4.

¹¹ We hardly need point out that this applies to the theory of the "*pratico-inerte*" in J. P. Sartre, *Critique de la raison dialectique*. Sartre misunderstands Marx's criticism of philosophy, ignores how it restores the sensuous, and represents a regression to Feuerbach's anthropology.

¹² Cf. MEGA, vol. III, pp. 111-44.

¹³ Marx's observations on need are scattered throughout his works, from the earliest (notably, the *Manuscripts of 1844*) to the latest. Cf. also the passage from *Critique of the Gotha Program* quoted on p. 179.

¹⁴ *Capital, op. cit.*, v. I, p. 87.

¹⁵ *Ibid.*, p. 96.

¹⁶ It may be noted in passing that Balzac gave us the best sociology of bourgeois society, taking his point of departure in the *Code Civil.*

¹⁷ *A Contribution to the Critique of Political Economy.* Trans. N. I. Stone. Chicago: Charles H. Kerr & Co., p. 55.

¹⁸ Marx's most significant text in this connection is the opening pages of *The Eighteenth Brumaire of Louis Bonaparte.*

¹⁹ Cf. particularly Marx's doctoral thesis on Epicurus and Democritus for its discussion of the materialism of these philosophers and their conception of freedom.

²⁰ Cf. the opening pages of the *Eighteenth Brumaire,* on historical acts which imitate the past, borrowing their costumes, gestures, and words from famous models.

²¹ MEGA, v. III, p. 121.

[22] Georges Gurvitch has pointed out several times, particularly in his mimeographed course of Sorbonne lectures, Marx's importance as a sociologist. He has argued his views against philosophical, economic, and historical dogmatisms. The position taken here differs somewhat from his. We do not believe that Marx's sociology is to be found almost exclusively in his early works. We think it is possible to discern a sociological aspect in *Capital*. Nor do we believe that Marx's sociology is primarily of retrospective interest, etc.

[23] It is hardly necessary to point out that Marx uses here the term "foundation" (*Grundlage*) to denote not an economic reality, but a sociological reality, a praxis which he clearly relates to a given historically determined level of productive forces. The social relations of personal dependency constitute the *structure*, i.e., the real "foundation" of medieval society.

[24] *Capital, op. cit.,* v. I, pp. 88–92.

[25] *Ibid.,* p. 81.

[26] *Die Deutsche Ideologie,* opening pages.

[27] *Ibid.,* MEGA, First Section, v. V, p. 424.

[28] *Ibid.,* p. 210.

[29] *Capital,* v. I, p. 103.

[30] *Ibid.*

[31] *Die Heilige Familie.* MEGA, First Section, v. III, p. 212.

[32] MEGA, vol. III, p. 129.

[33] This procedure may be likened to Husserl's "phenomenological reduction," which puts within brackets part or even the whole of the content of consciousness, also to Saussure's "semantic reduction" which distinguishes between language and the spoken words. But there is one important difference: Marx says explicitly that his reduction is on the plane of praxis, that it is not a mental operation but a real continuous dialectical process.

We must once again emphasize the fact that most interpreters of Marx's *Capital* have overlooked the importance of the concept of form in the fundamental theory of exchange value and the theory of the commodity. They give this concept a superficial meaning, such as it has in a sentence like "The cabinet maker gave the wood the form of a table, a chair." But Marx uses the term "form" in a rigorously defined sense, comparable to the sense it has in such phrases as "logical form" or "mathematical form." Marx says as well as shows that the form is a structure. Here we cannot pause to go into a number of problems, such as that of the relations obtaining between linguistic form and the commodity form. Historically there can be no doubt that the emergence of exchange value, i.e., of the commodity form, brought in its train the consciousness of language as a form—the Greek *logos* with its different usages and formal disciplines (logic, rhetoric, aophistics, grammar). Analysis of these relationships and interactions would require a specialized work. We do not propose to develop this theme here, we must limit ourselves to mentioning it. Book I of *Capital* is an admirable text but a difficult one; it is impossible to understand it in detail without thorough preparation. The best approach is obviously by way of Hegelianism. But any philosophical background—classical, phenomenological, even existentialist or structuralist—is better than no background at all. We may add that today, whatever the "approach" chosen, a new reading can be justified only by practical experience of the "modern" world and a sense of the need to elucidate it conceptually.

What is the source of the concept of "form" itself? The foundations of scientific knowledge were elaborated by philosophy, more particularly by logic and the logicians. Science borrowed this concept from philosophy by severing it from its speculative context in the systematized structures of classical philosophy. Those who do not understand this essential aspect of cognition inevitably fall into a scientistic positivism which views science as a collection of facts linked by arbitrary assertions, presuppositions, and postulates.

What we are saying here derives from a lengthy effort to restore formal considerations (formal logic, etc.) to dialectical thought: our aim is not a formalist or structuralist interpretation of Marxism.

[34] *Capital*, v. I, pp. 41–2.

[35] *Ibid.*

[36] *Ibid.*, p. 46.

[37] *Ibid.*, p. 56.

[38] *Ibid.*, p. 54. The last sentence was added by Marx to the French edition of the work.

[39] Continuing our analogy between the commodity and language, we may say that social labor is "paradigmatic" in relation to the commodity form. The form confers upon each thing the significance of a commodity and includes it in a "syntagmatic" whole (by relating it to other things). "Value, therefore, does not stalk about with a label describing what it is. It is value, rather, that converts every product into a social hieroglyphic. Later on, we try to decipher the hieroglyphic, to get behind the secret of our own social products; for to stamp an object of utility as a value is just as much a social product as language" (*Capital*, v. I, p. 85).

All this does not mean that commodities and money are mere signs, and yet, not only is there a language of commodities, but there is also magic in them as in current usage (cf. *Capital*, Book I, Chapter II).

[40] "*Qua* values, all commodities are expressions of one and the same unit, human labor, and interchangeable. Consequently, a commodity can be exchanged for another commodity whenever it has a form that makes it appear as a value." (Passage added by Marx to French version of *Capital*, Book I, 1, 3.)

[41] *Capital*, v. I, p. 83.

[42] This well-known thesis has been put forward by Georges Lukács, according to whom human relations are converted into things and relations among things.

[43] "The purchase of labor power for a fixed period is the prelude to the process of production; and this prelude is constantly repeated when the stipulated term comes to an end, when a definite period of production, such as a week or a month, has elapsed. But the laborer is not paid until he has expended his labor power, and realized in commodities not only its value, but surplus value. He has therefore produced not only surplus value, . . . but also, before it flows back to him in the shape of wages, the fund out of which he himself is paid, the variable capital. . . . What

flows back to the laborer in the shape of wages is a portion of the product that is continuously reproduced by him. . . . The transaction is veiled by the commodity form of the product and the money form of the commodity" (*Capital*, v. I, pp. 621–2).

⁴⁴ The most superficial of these interpretations characterizes the commodity psychologically, by its use value (desirability, power to give satisfaction). We have on the contrary emphasized the analogy between the commodity and the twofold nature of language and the sign. Lukács' theory of reification goes deeper, but fails to do justice to Marx's theoretical analysis of capitalism, and rules out any concrete sociology of bourgeois society (as well as its disappearance and transition to "something else").

⁴⁵ *Capital*, v. I, p. 809.

⁴⁶ *Ibid.*, v. III, p. 1031 (last chapter, unfinished, which was to contain a detailed analysis of classes under competitive capitalism).

⁴⁷ Who perhaps simplifies the thought of Adam Smith in his polemics. Cf. his remarks on A. Smith in *Theories of Surplus Value*.

⁴⁸ *Capital*, v. I, p. 558.

⁴⁹ K. Marx: *Theories of Surplus Value*. Trans. Emile Burns. Foreign Language Publishing House, Moscow. P. 376.

⁴⁹ᵃ *Ibid.*

⁵⁰ In *Selected Essays*, trans. H. J. Stenning. London, n.d. Leonard Parsons. P. 24.

⁵¹ *Ibid.*, pp. 24–5.

⁵² *Ibid.*, p. 50.

⁵³ *Ibid.*, pp. 55–6.

⁵⁴ *Ibid.*, p. 56.

⁵⁵ *Ibid.*, p. 60.

⁵⁶ *Ibid.*, p. 66.

⁵⁷ *Ibid.*, pp. 66–7.

⁵⁸ *Ibid.*, pp. 73–4.

⁵⁹ *Ibid.*, pp. 83–5.

⁶⁰ MEGA, First Section, v. I, pp. 401–553.

⁶¹ *Ibid.*, pp. 434–5.

⁶² *Ibid.*, p. 484. Translation by T. M. Knox (*Hegel's Philosophy of Right.* Oxford at the Clarendon Press, 1942. P. 197).

⁶³ MEGA, v. I, pp. 497 f., 550 f.

⁶⁴ *Hegel's Philosophy of Right, op. cit.*, p. 193.

⁶⁵ MEGA, v. V, p. 455.

⁶⁶ *Ibid.*

⁶⁷ *Ibid.*

⁶⁸ *Ibid.*

⁶⁹ *Ibid.*, p. 456.

⁷⁰ *Ibid.*

⁷¹ *Ibid.*

⁷² *Ibid.*, p. 461.

⁷³ *Ibid.*

⁷⁴ *Hegel's Philosophy of Right*, par. 295 (*op. cit.*, p. 192).

⁷⁵ MEGA, v. I, p. 463.

⁷⁶ *Ibid.*, p. 464.

⁷⁷ Letter to Ruge. MEGA, v. I, p. 574.

⁷⁸ *Poverty of Philosophy* (1845).

⁷⁹ *The Eighteenth Brumaire of Louis Bonaparte.* In K. Marx and F. Engels, *Selected Works.* Foreign Language Publishing House, Moscow, 1950, v. I, pp. 301–03.

⁸⁰ *Die Deutsche Ideologie.* MEGA, v. V, p. 307.

⁸¹ *Ibid.*, p. 176.

[82] We may add America before Columbus, and even afterward. Marx treated of the Asiatic mode of production in *Capital* (v. II, Book I), in his articles in the *New York Tribune* (Marx appeared frequently in the *Tribune* from 1851/62. The articles were often written in collaboration with Engels), in his correspondence with Engels, and in *Pre-Capitalist Modes of Production*. For one of the few occasions when official Marxism has displayed a degree of independence, see a recent discussion published in *La pensée*, April and October 1964.

[83] *Enthüllungen über den Kommunistenprozess zu Köln*. Basel and Boston, 1853.

[84] Letter to Bracke, May 5, 1875.

[85] *New York Tribune*, October 19, 1853.

[86] Speech at Amsterdam, 1872. Cf. G. Steckloff, *History of the First International*, English translation, p. 240.

[87] Taken from *The American Journalism of Marx and Engels*, New York, pp. 7–8.

[88] *The Class Struggles in France, 1848–1850*. In *Selected Works*, *op. cit.*, p. 204.

[89] Correspondence with Proudhon (May 1846).

Index

Index

About the Author

Henri Lefebvre was born in 1901 in Hagetmau, Landes, France. During the course of a long and distinguished career he has lectured around the world and has taught at the universities of Strasbourg and Paris-Nanterre. Professor Lefebvre has made important contributions to the fields of sociology, philosophy, political science, and literature. Among his books to have appeared in English translation are *The Sociology of Marx, Everyday Life in the Modern World,* and *The Survival of Capitalism.*